From the authors of
*Seven Deadly Diseases
of Ministry Marketing*

The
GOD of the
INTERNET

25 Scriptural Secrets for Raising
Ministry Money Online

BY DOUG BRENDEL
with E. Dale Berkey, Ph.D. & Jack W. Sheline

The God of the Internet

25 Scriptural Secrets for Raising
Ministry Money Online

by Doug Brendel

with E. Dale Berkey, Ph.D. & Jack W. Sheline

© 2000 *Berkey Brendel Sheline*

Published by Home & Family Publishers

Cover design by: J. David Ford & Associates
Hurst, Texas

International Standard Book Number: 0-9643164-0-4

BERKEY BRENDEL SHELINE
Ministry Development Specialists
60 Shiawassee, Suite G • Fairlawn, OH 44333

voice (330) 867-5224 • fax (330) 869-5607

email servant@berkeybrendelsheline.com

www.berkeybrendelsheline.com

Contents

I. FIVE SECRETS OF THE RIVER

Life is fluid; change is natural. It's also good — because it's God's way of bringing growth.

The bedrock principles of God's design never change; but the techniques of fulfilling that design must continually change.

The Internet is not a substitute for God's provision or God's guidance.

God looks for, and finds, people where they are — He doesn't make them come to Him.

To go into a new land, you have to clear customs. To fulfill a God-given vision, you must adapt in order to communicate effectively.

II. FIVE SECRETS OF COMMUNICATION

God places a priority on quality communication, because it's a prerequisite to persuasion, conviction, response, and change.

Listening and the feedback that comes from it are every bit as valuable as talking and preaching. Giving the other person the opportunity to set their receptors to the ideal frequency, and then to speak their mind in response, is a manifestation of love. Love is practical.

Even though God looks for people rather than waiting for

them to look for Him, He reaches out to them through us. It's not automatic; we have to get the word out.

God cares more about people than He does about programs, institutions, trends, or even religions.

God is no respecter of demographics. He loves everybody the same. But Jesus spoke to people, and won them over, on the basis of their uniqueness. He has given us, in the Internet, an opportunity to reach a wider variety of people "types" — yet speak to each in his or her own language.

III. Five Secrets of Relationship

Whatever you value, you invest in; whatever you invest in pays dividends. Whatever you don't invest in won't pay dividends. If you're not investing in it, you don't value it — regardless of how strongly you insist otherwise.

Money follows ministry, not the other way around. And ministry is relationship. Focus on relationship, God will enable ministry, and money can follow. Relationship is the key. People reward it; God values it.

I need to learn to think about the other person's needs, not just my own.

God values long-term relationship. This is the essence of biblical community.

For maximum effectiveness, count the cost; gauge your impact.

IV. Five Secrets of Identity

God gave you the vision for your ministry. Keep that picture clearly in focus. But as you communicate that picture to people, you must communicate in terms they can understand.

V. FIVE SECRETS OF THE HARVEST

He's Got a Secret

Is there a God of the Internet?

And if there is, is He the same God as *our* God?

Yes, indeed.

Perhaps it seems irreverent to refer to God as a computer expert — it doesn't seem very "holy," does it?

But the fact is, our Lord knows more about computers than Bill Gates and Steven Jobs combined.

We tend to think of the Internet as new, and God as old. In a way, we have it backwards. God foresaw computers back before Noah learned to count animals. The dawn of the Internet was no surprise to God. To Him, it's old news.

And the future of the Internet doesn't make God nervous a bit. God is freshly involved in every new day of our lives ... every technological twist we come up with.

He wove into the brains of human beings the thrilling capacity for invention. It was God who thought up the concept of binary code. It was God who first visualized computers talking to each other. It was God who conceived of the great gulf between PC users and Macintosh devotees. (Did He giggle? Or just shake His head and sigh?)

For Christ-followers committed to building God's kingdom, the Internet poses challenges, questions, opportunities, and risks. For some, the Age of the Internet is a threat. What's a baud rate? And why, after nailing a master's degree in biblical languages, should anyone care? For others, the Age of the Internet seems like utopia — finally, a way to communicate with more people more cheaply and get more feedback more quickly!

The truth, however, is somewhere in between "I

don't need no stinkin' Internet" and "This will solve all my ministry problems."

How to get at this truth — without going back to college for a degree in computer science — is the great question of our day. Authors, speakers, and a variety of self-styled guru-geeks are offering to teach us gigabytes of stuff about the Internet ... more than we could possibly want or need to know. A zillion books, videos, audio tapes, and CDs have already flooded the market — they're clogging bookstores, catalogs, even the Internet itself. (What does it mean when you order a book over the Internet that teaches you how to order a book over the Internet?)

This book, we can only hope, offers something different. Here's what we have in mind:

We, the authors, are ministry development specialists who have devoted our lives to building Christian organizations through scripturally sound marketing strategies. We have confirmed, over the course of nearly three-quarters of a century of combined labor, that God's Word really does apply — practically, specifically, and unilaterally — to any and every facet of human life and work.

So when we saw the Internet tidal wave heading our way, we ran for the same lifeboat we've always run to: God's Word.

Desperate for answers (because, after all, we are accountable to God for the marketing success of more than three dozen Christian ministries at any given time), we began searching the Scriptures for timeless truths — and asking God to show us ways to apply those truths to the rampant, ever-changing world of Internet technology.

In a number of ways, the results surprised us. On the other hand, we shouldn't have been surprised at all. The secrets to Internet fundraising that we found in the Bible were only secrets to us, not to God. He designed our universe by them. They are truths ... they are *truth*. They have always been — and will always be — totally true. That means they still apply today, in the Age of the Internet.

Here, then, are 25 scriptural secrets to advancing the Kingdom of God while raising money via the Internet for your ministry. ("Seek first his kingdom and his righteousness, and all these things will be given to you as well," Jesus assures us in Matthew 6:33.) We've tried to arrange "SpeedLinks" and other time-saving helps along the way, in hopes of getting you most efficiently to the information you want and need.

Any of a number of sources can teach you how to use the Internet, how to "do ministry" via the Internet, even how to raise money for a ministry or charity on the Internet. But only if we take the truth of God's Word and apply it to our online marketing strategies will we be truly successful, in the whole sense of the term — not just making money, but making our ministries more like Christ's ideal.

We do know this: God loves people; that's why the Internet happened. The Internet is a gift from God, a tool for spreading the Good News. It can help people find real love, truth, and hope, which leads to a better life. This is a priority for God. Throughout history He has enabled people to invent new means of helping people. Only mankind has often corrupted their uses.

Our prayer is that, as we strive to apply these truths to the marketing of our ministries, God will honor your commitment and ours to Him and to His Word ... and we will see the cause of Christ flourishing around the world as a result.

We welcome your feedback. Our web address is www.berkeybrendelsheline.com, our email address is servant@berkeybrendelsheline.com, our fax is

330.869.5607, our phone is 330.867.5224, our street address is 60 Shiawassee Avenue, Suite G, Fairlawn, Ohio 44333.

I.
FIVE SECRETS OF THE RIVER

〰⟲ SpeedLink:

This section is for YOU if ...
- You wonder whether the Internet is part of **God's will** for your ministry
- You're unsure about **the future** of the Internet
- You're **frustrated with fundraising** and hope the Internet can help in a big way *fast*
- You feel uneasy about all the new Internet-related **"lingo"**

When Niagara Changes Course

Scriptural Secret #1:
Life is fluid; change is natural. It's also good — because it's God's way of bringing growth.

When it began to be evident that charitable organizations might raise funds via the Internet, many charities (Christian and non) were reluctant to go there. It was too scary, or too risky, or too much work, or whatever. Many simply felt we were quite a number of years away from seeing any serious money travel into nonprofit organizations by way of the Internet.

Those who fully understood the potential, however, were going crazy.

David M. Lawson, president of the Prospect Information Network and a specialist in raising money for colleges, declared in the *Chronicle of Higher Education*: "We are artificially suppressing the amount of money

that could be raised. We are in a Niagara Falls of money
... I want to pull my hair out. Get a bucket, and get under
there."

While it doesn't really seem that a "Niagara Falls of
money" is flowing over the Internet — at least not yet —
certainly there *are* financial resources flowing into
ministries. And *some* of it — more and more of it — will
flow into ministries over the Internet.

**What we often forget about Niagara Falls is that
it's actually just a *huge step down* in the Niagara River.
Likewise, if there is ever going to be a Niagara Falls
of donations flowing over the Internet, it will
be because the Niagara *River* of donations got re-
channeled.**

**And that's what's puzzling or troubling or nerve-
wracking to many ministry marketers today: The river
of funding is shifting its course.**

A river flows through a channel of earth, rock, and
sand. It seems to flow more or less along exactly the
same route day after day, year after year. But in reality,
the route of the river is always changing, at least
gradually. Various factors — the hardness of the rock
that forms the channel, for example, or the wind
direction and velocity — nudge the water-flow against
the edges of the channel. Gradually the pressure of this
nudged water carves out new routes, usually for just a
portion of the water.

Ministry marketers have always found this to be
true of the river of financial resources flowing into
Christian organizations. A disaster relief organization,
for example, may have raised a lot of funds over the
years by way of bright yellow urgent-format mailings —
but now find that the rate of response to this format is
slacking off.

What changed? A million details, perhaps.

Maybe donors have been saturated with bright

yellow urgent-format mailings so this type of package arriving in the mailbox simply doesn't have the impact it once had?

Or maybe with more information available via TV and the Internet, the donors have come to crave more detail, in the way of a brochure or newsletter or other insert, before they decide to give?

Or maybe charity scandals in the news have led donors to become more skeptical of the organization — maybe the yellow urgent-format package triggers some subliminal (even if unfair) connection to those scandals in the donor's mind?

The wise ministry marketer has recognized all along that *every single impression* made on a donor by *any medium whatsoever* has the effect of *changing* the donor's perceptions, even if only slightly. The common wisdom is that "**the marketplace is always shifting under us,**" like the tectonic plates of the earth's crust.

The practical result is that some portion of the money given by donors to ministries *shifts*. It is now given to a different cause, or it is given in greater or smaller volume, or it is given at a different frequency. The riverbed is being chipped away in one direction or another.

Rivers can change course suddenly, too. Sometimes a tree falls, or a boulder tumbles down a mountain, and the water is forced to re-route itself suddenly. **Ask anyone who was raising funds for ministries back when the Jim Bakker and Jimmy Swaggart scandals occurred, and they will recall only too painfully the fallen-tree-or-avalanche effect**. In a seeming instant, with a horrible crash, the river of ministry funding can seem to dam up — or roar over and around the obstacle, digging a new channel into other ministries or causes.

Mapmakers, geologists, and others make it their business to monitor rivers' movements both massive and minute. Often, they can tell you in advance where a river is likely to head. Sometimes, they get fooled; the water moves, and changes, too fast.

Viewed from the standpoint of all the charitable contributions given in, say, a year's time, the Internet appears to be gradually chipping away at the riverbank, slowly moving more and more funds into the online channel. Nothing to panic about. Get on the Internet when you can; everything is going to be all right.

But viewed from the standpoint of *how* charitable contributions have been given *historically* — over, say, our lifetime — the Internet begins to look like a colossal boulder crashing down from above without warning.

Throughout our lives, each new method of giving has taken less and less time to "catch on." Contributions were given largely in person (at churches), and largely in cash , throughout most of our childhood. Gradually a larger percentage of contributions were given by mail, by check or by money order.

Then, in just the past 25 years, credit cards swept into play. Suddenly you could respond to a radio or television offer by picking up your phone, dialing toll-free, and giving instantly. Telemarketing sprang up quickly, and grew enormously in a relatively short period of time. As recently as 1995, it was rare to find a way to give a charitable contribution online . But the rate-of-change curve is bending dramatically upward.

There's a stereotype, not entirely unfair, in the Church at large, which is marked by resistance to change. Many of us — comfy and cozy in the warm, fuzzy blanket of "We've always done it this way" — will have to be dragged kicking and screaming into the Age of the Net.

We don't like change. We're more comfortable where we are, with what we have, than in dabbling with the unknown. One well known ministry development specialist, uneasy about cyberspace, dictates his memos via voicemail, where they're transcribed by a secretary and emailed out — all on a strict 24-hour deadline, the slowest email in America. Well known pastor Bill Hybels chuckles about his elder board offering him a fancy computer as a perk of his office. "They know I'm computer-illiterate," Hybels says, so of course he'll politely decline. "They're just playing a little game with me!"

I confess to the change-resistance syndrome myself. When I began working as a writer in 1976, I delighted in writing my first drafts longhand on yellow legal pads. The efficiency expert William E. Coad assured me I would never excel unless I learned to compose at the typewriter. I'm a very fast typist, but I resisted his advice — until one day, an out-of-control deadline forced me to plunge into the first draft of a book project at my clackity old Royal typewriter. Soon a friend was insisting I get an electric typewriter, which I also resisted as long as I could. When word processing became available, Dale Berkey urged me to grow up and get one. When the Macintosh computer made its splash, Dale actually *bought* me one to get me into the modern era. Then it was a case of "My dot-matrix printer is fine; a laser printer is too expensive." Then it was "What's a modem?" "What? You don't have email?" "What? You don't have a website?" "What? You don't have your own domain name?"

Today, I look back on this litany of strange new terms and I shrug. But as each one invaded my life, it made my upper lip sweat. It was "technology." I imagined it was smarter than I was. I imagined it would make me look like a fool. I imagined — worst of all — that I would spend a lot of money on it and then turn out *not to need it!*

But the fact is, we do need change. Change is a

blessing, not a curse. We must change. **Students of history tell us that civilizations are wiped out because of their failure to adapt to new circumstances — or grow powerful because of their embrace of change. This is not just happenstance; it is God's design.**

Change is often — maybe even usually — painful. But pain is the most effective growth device in the world. The apostle Paul observes in **Romans 5:3,4** that we can "rejoice in our sufferings, because we know that suffering produces perseverance; perseverance, character; and character, hope." He's mapping out the ideal spiritual growth curve of the Christ-follower's life. To make me more like Christ, more like God's ideal for me, He starts with a secret ingredient: | *pain* | !

The challenge of change has an equally potent side-effect: It more or less forces us to keep turning back to God for direction. When Jesus in **Luke 18** tells the parable of the pushy widow and the unjust judge, He holds up the ideal of talking with God about our problems "day and night." Many cling to the promise of the parable — that God will meet needs — without taking note of the fact that Jesus isn't giving us carte blanche. The promise of this parable is for His followers who are willing to "always pray and not give up" (**Luke 18:1**), "who cry out to him day and night" (**Luke 18:7**).

The Internet is a wonderful source of pain, because it's more than just new: It's ever-new. It's a constant source of the character-building pain of change! (Somebody say "Hooray.") Internet technology in effect feeds on itself. Every new detail of computer technology ripples through the Internet, forcing adjustments in the way we use it — and affecting every other form of communication in our lives: telephone, television, radio, music, church services, you name it. So this isn't just the latest fad that we can get a handle on and camp out with — the way we switched from the mimeograph machine to the photocopier. While document-duplicating strategies have morphed slowly over the years, Internet strategies will morph over months, or even weeks — because the technology is advancing so quickly.

In fact, significant changes have occurred between the time we began writing this book and the time you're reading it. In the ideal universe, we wouldn't have even printed this book on paper. We only printed it in this form so that you could read it on a boat on a lake on your vacation, or on an airplane (although you'd be able to read a book like this "online" on an airplane, or via satellite on your houseboat, with the proper equipment — which is already available).

Because of the breakneck pace of change in InternetLand, this book really must be updated _continuously_. Which is why we have posted it on the Internet — and why we are updating it at least once a month. When you buy this book (which can only happen online), you actually buy a one-year _subscription_ to the book. You get a unique password which allows you to "visit" the book online, at <u>www.berkeybrendelsheline.com/internet</u>. From there you can read, download, use, and file all the latest news and information that impacts or overrides the details you originally found in this book.

Scriptural Secret #2:

The bedrock principles of God's design never change; but the techniques of fulfilling that design must continually change.

There is no 67th Book of Marketing in the Bible.

There are only 66 books. They're what we have to live by; they're what we have to minister by.

The marketing of our ministries — with or without the Internet — must happen according to the same principles by which we live our lives. As we said in our 1999 book *The Seven Deadly Diseases of Ministry Marketing*, wherever we don't align with the design by which God created us, there's going to be a sense of disquiet. **First Peter 1:5** calls us to conform to God's design in *all* we do. There are no footnotes excusing or excluding ministry marketers.

Some things never change. God's Word, for example, isn't going anywhere. It's staying put. Even in this world of chaotic change, it won't be moved. The principles by which God designed the universe are locked in.

But that's just hardware. Throughout human history we see God's continuous updating of the software. Before there was a Temple, how did people worship? Then there was a Temple — but then there wasn't again. God spoke through mankind's mouths for who knows how long? Then He directed His Word to be written on scrolls. When Gutenberg started cranking out multiple copies on his first press, God didn't flinch; He had to be glad! Marconi invented the "wireless," and pretty soon somebody thought to read Scripture on the radio . Billy Graham did big crusade meetings promoted through newspapers . Rex Humbard and Oral Roberts pioneered weekly television ministry. (Humbard trusted God, outrageously, to give him a *weekly global* outreach — before there was such a thing as satellite communication — or even videotape duplication!) Today various Christian organizations are accomplishing truly effective ministry by way of film , video and audio tape, CDs and DVDs , and yes, the Internet .

God's Word still reads the same. But the techniques for communicating it have changed from era to era.

To serve on the cutting edge of a new ministry technique can be difficult. Opinions are deeply divided, for example, on the future of broadcast television. Broadcast veteran Jerry Rose took a beating when he engineered the morphing of Chicago's Christian TV station into a "content provider" — Internet Age terminology for an entity that *produces* programs rather than *distributes* programs. TV38 had been one of the nation's foremost Christian TV stations — but by the late 90s, a local broadcast station represented only one of *numerous* vehicles for distributing programs. Other outstanding Christian television stations have shifted with good success into networking, program production, and other strategies. Meanwhile, with the proliferation of videotape, CD-ROM, the Internet, cable, satellite, and on and on, Rose and his ministry board determined to make a change, too — but some longtime supporters howled. "God gave us this station as a sacred trust!" they cried. Not so, Rose responded. **The Gospel is a sacred trust. The rest is just technology — and the technology will mutate from age to age.**

Ministries need to use their funds wisely, doing what is most effective. In the strangest story Jesus ever told, in **Luke 16**, the wasteful company manager faces the prospect of an audit — and certain termination. We expect him either to throw himself on the master's mercy or get fired as he deserves. But neither happens. The squanderer's response to his dilemma is to offer deep discounts to prime customers, to get on their good side before the audit takes place.

Then, of course, we're *sure* he's going to get a vicious reprimand from the boss. But again, Jesus as storyteller twists the plot unexpectedly. The owner shows up and *applauds* the wasteful manager — for being *crafty!* The manager was using whatever techniques he could *today* in order to achieve good results *later.*

Likewise, Jesus says in **Luke 16:9**, "Use worldly wealth to gain friends for yourselves, so that when it is gone, you will be welcomed into eternal dwellings."

Use the Internet, Jesus is saying — or laser-disks, or satellites, or whatever you can get your hands on — if using that technology will draw people into relationship with you, and with Christ.

We tend to want Jesus to be stricter than He was. We want Him to ban the techniques we're not comfortable with. I have friends in ministry who will raise money for their cause via fish fries but *never* by telephone. I have other friends in ministry who will raise money for their cause via telemarketing but *never* by staging fish fries. Perhaps telemarketing is repugnant to you. If so, fine. (Fish fries are repugnant to *me*.) Let's just not suggest that one technique or another is somehow unscriptural or unspiritual because we don't *like* it.

Many will avoid raising money via the Internet because they see it as a huge expense. But moving your ministry's bucket under the flow of Internet donations is absolutely crucial — because of how the river is shifting. **Some 100 million Americans are using the Internet**, according to Cyberatlas (www.cyberatlas.com).

On a single day (11/14/99), according to Nielsen (www.nielsen-netratings.com), Americans spent a total of 10.8 million hours online from *home alone* — not including workplace access!

Time magazine's board of economists said in the magazine's October 4, 1999, issue, "The Internet will transform nearly everything, mostly for good." Revenues of the "Internet economy" passed the $300 billion mark in 1998, and were on target to *double* before the end of 1999. Dramatically more commercial sales occur online every year. Online consumer spending is expected to approach $25 billion in 2000 and $80 billion by 2003. According to some estimates, 22 million people will be *banking* online by 2002. And major nonprofit organizations (because they're already well known) are already raising millions via the Internet.

The American Red Cross raised almost $14 million in the month of April 1999 alone during the Kosovo refugee crisis — $1 million of which came online.

World Vision was raising $183,000 a month online during the Kosovo refugee crisis.

By the summer of 1999, Second Harvest was raising about $18,000 in cash and $67,000 in donated product per month.

That same summer, one Christian radio station — holding a "sharathon" fundraising drive simultaneously on the air and online — took in 13% of their commitments online.

Online giving is by no means limited to conservative Christian causes. The ACLU had 200,000 hits within 48 hours of President Bill Clinton's signing of the Telecommunications Bill (which the organization opposed strenuously). In three months the site had generated $25,000 in contributions, before giving leveled off as the big telecommunications news story grew stale.

It's already too late to decline raising money online

by claiming that too many people fear loss of privacy, or just plain loss ("Someone might get my credit card number!"). Fear of buying online is diminishing, particularly as more and more people come to understand "secure" transactions (where data flows in what amounts to "secret code" between the buyer and seller).

In fact, it is easier than ever to establish a secure connection for charitable donation's over a ministry's website. (Berkey Brendel Sheline can help you with this, via www.berkeybrendelsheline.com. On the other hand, don't even *try* to get a donor's credit card information via standard email or a non-secured web page. The percentage of people willing to give credit card numbers over the Internet without adequate security is so small as to be non-existent. Security makes all the difference between getting the gift and not getting it.)

After Harvard Law School became one of the first major colleges to enable donors to give online, Michael Stoner, vice-president for new media at Lipman Hearne, a Chicago-based marketing and fundraising company, observed that enabling donors to give via the Internet "sends a very practical and very symbolic statement. Practically, giving online allows a donor to close the loop right then and there. Symbolically, it says, 'I'm hip.' I think among young donors, there is a competitive advantage to [Harvard] being one of the first colleges to do this."

(If you're uneasy about people who might visit your ministry via the Internet and want to give but are still reluctant to do so online, add a print-out-able contribution form to your ministry website, which can be mailed in with a check.)

"Online or obsolete," a USA *Today* headline declared as long ago as 1999. "To web or not to Web? is not the question," says Peggy Pulliam, general manager of electronic commerce for R.R. Donnelley's online services, "but rather: When and how to Web?"

The fact is, your ministry *must* have a presence on the Internet. Otherwise your ministry will miss out, even disappear, as more and more communication activity in our society occurs via Internet instead of via other means.

Direct mail, TV, telemarketing, even live events — like church services, and the offerings you receive during them — are converging.

The Internet can do it all. And because it can, it will.

Indeed, the Bill Gateses of the world of course are working on a box that will provide all of these functions at once, easily.

The Internet, then, is not just about businesses trying to make a profit, or pornographers trying to ply their trade. The Internet is about spreading the Good News. It's about churches (people moving to a new community are church-shopping via the Internet), parachurch ministries (volunteers, donors, and even staff are being recruited via the Internet), schools (high schoolers are picking their colleges, for example, via the Internet), even families!

Families? Yes. And not just helping your fourth-grader find information on the Ming Dynasty for a school report. Many families have discovered that the Internet is literally a means to greater communication and bonding across even international boundaries. They don't send cards and letters anymore: They "post" photographs and messages on their private family website, where any member of the family can access the latest stuff from anywhere on the planet!

Even more unnerving for many church leaders is the growing number of people, mostly youthful, who are *attending church* online. Whether we like it or not, many church-shoppers are essentially saying, "Why not?" A church can set up a simple video camera to capture its services, then (with relatively simple Internet technology) route that live image to the church's site on the Internet — where anybody can experience it simultaneously. For those who miss it, it can be made "downloadable" by anyone at any time.

Will the river change course? It's already — and always — changing! Our challenge is to figure out how, and when, to get our ministries into the flow!

Scriptural Secret #3:

The internet is not a substitute for God's provision or God's guidance.

I have a friend — let's call him Smith — who is a notorious over-spender. In spite of the fact that he's rapidly approaching retirement age, he does not save; he does not invest. He frequently begins a sentence with the phrase, "When my ship comes in ..." Yet Smith has actually missed the boat. He subsists on a vague belief that someday, somehow, his financial picture will improve.

I have another friend — let's call him Jones — a church pastor, who actually plays the lottery, hoping to bring his church a windfall someday!

Perhaps we snicker at both of these guys. But maybe we're more like them than we realize, or want to think about. Does the thought of taking your ministry marketing effort to the Internet cause your heart to pound with eager anticipation? Do you imagine tons of new donors, big donors, lifetime donors, flooding into your ministry via your new ministry website? Do the nervous types — those who are reluctant to get their ministries on the Internet — make you feel smug and superior?

Oops. Maybe you're Smith or Jones after all.

For people comfortable with the idea of the Internet, it can be intoxicating — a seeming panacea for every ill. Business owners have shuttered their retail stores and moved totally to the Internet — only to struggle or even die. Entrepreneurs have launched Internet enterprises, confident that their Big Idea, once posted to the Internet, would make them the next billionaire of the Net Age — only to be cruelly disappointed.

The massive Time Warner media conglomerate, which more than just about any other entity should have been able to succeed in a communications medium, launched its imposing Pathfinder megamedia site on the Internet in October 1994. They invested an estimated $150 million before it had "slumped off the charts." By mid-1999, Pathfinder was "slated for deconstruction"

The lesson to be learned in the midst of all this destruction? There is no free lunch. The Internet is not a cure-all for your ministry fundraising problems — any more than *anything* is a cure-all for your ministry fundraising problems.

In our ministries, we must not only be "wise as serpents" — employing scientific research in our construction of Internet strategies — but we must also recognize that God, not technology, is our source of supply.

Solomon's advice still applies, thousands of years later, in the Internet Age: If I want my ministry to have long life and prosperity, I need to live by **Proverbs 3:5-7**: "Trust in the Lord with all your heart and lean not on your own understanding; in all your ways acknowledge him, and he will make your paths straight. Do not be wise in your own eyes...."

The result, he says in verse 8, will be "health to your body and nourishment to your bones" — both of which we ardently wish for our ministries.

Over-dependence on the Internet is a symptom of under-dependence on God. And one common sign of that deadly over-dependence is an unrealistically rosy view of how Internet exposure will improve life in the organization.

Commercial businesses have found out the hard

way, for example, that the Internet isn't a simpler, cheaper way to do business. "It isn't cheaper to build" an online business, notes Fred Goss in a review of a profile in the *New York Times.* "It isn't cheaper to run."

What it *is*, for one thing, is hard work.

The attention that must be given to an Internet site is significant — and constant. As we shall see, a site can't simply be posted and left to "do its thing." This is a formula for guaranteed failure.

Moreover, the Internet doesn't replace direct mail, live events, telemarketing, or any other existing strategies. It works in synch with them.

"Even nonprofits that are successfully making money now over the Internet," says Anna Couey in *MicroTimes,* "still rely heavily on traditional methods of fundraising to keep themselves going."

The advantage of the Internet, then, isn't that it streamlines our overall marketing effort (it actually makes it more complex), or that it makes our overall marketing effort less expensive (it actually costs money to get going). The primary advantage of the Internet right now is that it's growing — and that it has tremendous *potential* for reaching multitudes inexpensively.

"The Internet," Couey observes, "appears to solve many of the problems that direct mail campaigns face: Cost of entry is comparatively low, so that even small nonprofits can use the Internet to reach a greater number of people than they could possibly afford in any other medium."

Furthermore, *without* an Internet site, your ministry communicates a certain backwardness that isn't good for donor relations. **If someone hears about your ministry and can't find you on the Internet, you have inadvertently communicated to that prospective donor that you are old-fashioned, inefficient, and**

unworthy of her contributions.

(And if she finds you but she can't give to you online because your site hasn't provided the means, she has similar negative feelings — but they're even more detrimental to your ministry, because she *was* prepared to become a donor!)

So if the Internet isn't an automatic source of mega-bucks for your ministry, how have certain charities raised so much money online?

The big sites making money are the sites posted by charities that are "known" already. Their Internet sites, then, are simply convenient collection devices for people who are already aware of their organizations.

The widely known humanitarian organization CARE, for example, got $190,000 in 11 days during the Kosovo crisis, according to Marilyn Grist, CARE's vice-president for external relations, interviewed in the *NonProfit Times'* Direct Marketing Edition in May 1999. Many Internet users may have responded to the Kosovo news stories by visiting CARE's website (www.CARE.org). But CARE also wisely capitalized on this potential, by revising its website immediately to focus on the Kosovo crisis.

But the fact that CARE was well known *before* Kosovo shouldn't cause despair in less well known charitable organizations. Any ministry or nonprofit organization can adapt the same approach: Make some connection in your ministry site with "what's hot" in current events, and you may increase the number of "hits," or visits, from people browsing the Internet.

Even though Internet does not magically solve our ministry marketing problems, it does present spectacularly positive possibilities. With Internet exposure, your ministry can make more friends . It can increase its revenues . It can get information to donors more quickly. It can establish and strengthen relationships with donors. It can deepen donors' relationships more quickly than ever before. It can enable you to test, cost-effectively, donors' perceptions of your various projects, campaigns, and appeals.

If we rely on God's leading — seeing Him, and not the technology, as our source of supply — we have the opportunity to advance our ministries dramatically by way of the Internet.

As we shall see.

Scriptural Secret #4:

God looks for, and finds, people where they are — He doesn't make them come to Him.

The TV show you loved as a kid? You can probably download highlights of it in *seconds* today — via the Internet.

That software program you paid 600 bucks for? A few short years from now, you may find yourself using software *exclusively via the Internet* — without ever actually installing the application on your computer.

We think of TV, music, news, entertainment, and computer programs as having changed so much over the course of our lifetime — and sure, the content is different. But the most dramatic changes have come in *how we get the content.*

People are spending their time differently today than they were when we were kids — even differently than they were just five years ago! Just look at the remarkable changes in how we spend our time — and *how we access information.*

People don't just watch TV. They don't even just pop in a video. Now they "log on." "Check their email." "Surf the Net." "Shop online."

Millions of people today are spending way more time on the Internet than they spend opening and reading their mail — which, with the advent of email, is known derisively as "snail mail."

People today spend proportionately less time watching TV than they did when we were kids. The big networks are scrambling to keep profits up in the face of dwindling market share. What's pushing ABC, CBS, NBC,

Fox, and the newer upstarts into panic mode? The personal computer. The PC is becoming the primary information and entertainment unit of people's lives.

The numbers are literally incalculable because they change so quickly. By the end of 1999, according to *Fundraising on the Internet* (www.fundraisingonline.com), nearly two-thirds of all households with $40,000+ incomes had home computers. Some charitable organizations were reporting that more than a third of their donors had email addresses. With satellite and wireless technology already considered "old hat," Internet links have become a simple affair even for Bedouins in remote desert tents and sailors far out at sea!

All of which must be supremely pleasing to God — because He has always reached out to people, rather than force them to come searching for Him. David exulted in God's willingness to pursue people: "He parted the heavens and came down," he sang in **Psalm 18:9**. "He reached down from on high and took hold of me," he proclaimed in **2 Samuel 22:17**. Gideon was hiding (**Judges 6:11**). Moses was out tending sheep on the far side of the desert (**Exodus 3:1**). Paul was "on the road" (**Acts 26:13**). Jesus "found" Philip and called him to service (**John 1:43**). After healing the man at the Pool of Bethesda, Jesus "found" him at the temple (**John 5:14**) to spur him on in his spiritual growth. God reaches out to people faithfully. Even when we spurn Him, He remains available to us.

In this way, **the Internet beautifully reflects the heart of God**. It is on the brink of becoming a means of outreach to the entire human population. On a relative scale, it is cheap — the horrifying thing for Big Business is that so much of it is *free* — and getting cheaper all the time. Best of all, it's there 24 hours a day, simply waiting for anyone and everyone to check in.

When we come to see the Internet as a provision from God's heart, a means of fulfilling His longings for mankind, it will profoundly affect the way we approach the Internet, and the marketing of our ministries on it.

Scriptural Secret #5:

To go into a new land, you have to clear customs. To fulfill a God-given vision, you must adapt in order to communicate effectively.

You don't have to be a computer geek to present your ministry effectively on the Internet.

But it does help to understand the basics of how the Internet works — the "customs" of this strange new land — and some of the fundamental terms and phrases related to it.

It takes a little effort, but then effort for the sake of ministry is a valuable spiritual discipline. The apostle Paul made this effort when he switched from culture to culture. "To the Jews I became like a Jew, to win the Jews," he reminisced in **1 Corinthians 9:20-22**. "To those under the law I became like one under the law (though I myself am not under the law), so as to win those under the law. To those not having the law I became like one not having the law (though I am not free from God's law but am under Christ's law), so as to win those not having the law. To the weak I became weak, to win the weak. I have become all things to all men so that by all possible means I might save some."

If we learn the customs — how to communicate and function in cyberspace — we have the chance to reach millions who journey there. They, then, receive the benefit of the Gospel. Our ministries, along the way, become more effective. Paul himself recognized that he wasn't just doing this for others, but for his own sake as well: "I do all this for the sake of the gospel, *that I may share in its blessings*" (**1 Corinthians 9:23**).

Learning the customs of the Internet — "clearing

customs," if you will — may feel intimidating. But in the same way that a foreign country seems far more accessible on your second visit than it did on your first, the whole concept of the Internet is actually simpler than it may seem at first. We can nail down the basics in the next five minutes or so.

(For definitions of words and phrases related to the Internet, you may want to let the Internet itself teach you. You can visit NetLingo at www.netlingo.com, or Webopedia at www.webopedia.com. These sites provide a handy resource for any words or phrases that trip you up.)

Of course, if you're already up to speed on Internet tech and terminology, then skip this section.

But for the rest of us, here's the Internet in plain English.

• • •

Your computer has all kinds of files on it (you knew this). Somebody else's computer has all kinds of files on it (you knew this, too). You can get those files from one computer to the other by way of a regular old telephone line.

Two computers talking to each other over a phone line are said to be "online."

There's a little machine that translates files (words and images and whatever) into blips that can be conducted over that phone line. It can also "hear" blips coming over the phone line from another computer, and de-code them back into usable files. This little machine is called a modem. Modems can be *really* little — small enough to fit *inside* your computer, where you never even see it; you only operate it by way of your regular computer keyboard, via on-screen commands. But modems are also often separate units that sit near your computer, connected to it by a cable.

The "blips" that your files are translated into and

out of aren't called blips, at least not by geeks. They're called code. The code is measured in bits and bytes, kilobytes (abbreviated kb), megabytes (abbreviated MB), gigabytes (abbreviated GB), and so on. The challenge faced by the tech wizards is to get multitudinous gigabytes of code to zip hither and yon throughout the Internet at faster and faster rates. This is why a fast modem is more valuable than a slow one. It does the necessary translating and de-coding work. (At the end of the 20th century, your average Joe thought he had a reasonably fast modem if it was "56K," which means 56,000 bps. What's "bps"? Bits per second. That's a lot of bits in a pretty short time. Pretty fast.)

The geeky way of asking how fast someone's modem works is to say "What's your baud rate?" Why is it called a baud rate? I don't know.

To read, store, process, and manipulate all the text and images of the Internet Age requires a whole lot of computing power. Your computer probably can't do it. So you hire an ISP, or Internet Service Provider, to help you. (Our agency, for example, hired Mindspring, via www.mindspring.com.) The ISP has *massive* computers that it makes available to its customers. These mammoth computing machines are called "servers" (which is only appropriate, since each one serves a large number of other computers, like yours). Your server can actually be located anywhere, since everything "happens" over phone lines; it doesn't have to be situated close to your home or office.

When you "log on" to the Internet, your computer's modem is actually calling up your ISP's "server." Most ISP's arrange to have local dial-up numbers available to their customers, so your computer is placing a call that's "free" to you because you already have local phone service — or you're dialing a toll-free number the ISP has set up.

When you write an email message and send it, it actually goes to your ISP's "server" computer; it's stored there, then the server transmits it, usually within a few seconds, from there. (If you want, you can tell your email program to save a copy of your outbound email messages on your own computer.)

When you receive an email message from someone else, that message has actually gone from their computer (where they typed it), through their modem and over the phone line into their ISP's server, then over the phone lines to *your* ISP's server, and finally over the phone line to *your* modem and into *your* computer.

Likewise, if you have an Internet site, it's stored on an ISP's server. When someone in Upper Saddle River, New Jersey, visits your site, they are actually looking at text and images stored on the server computer owned and operated by your ISP. Our agency's Internet site, www.berkeybrendelsheline.com, is stored on Mindspring's server. When you type in our Internet address in the "browser" program on your computer, it tracks that address to its proper location at Mindspring, and within seconds reveals on your computer screen the words and images we've stored there for you.

You pay a fee, typically on a monthly basis, to your ISP. In exchange, under the most common kind of deal, you get a certain number of hours "online." So your computer can call up the server, send and receive email, upload new stuff to your website, browse other people's websites, whatever — and *not hang up* in between functions.

Many ISPs sell unlimited online time as part of their deal, which is how many people stay online all day long. (You can tell most email programs to check for new messages as often as every 60 seconds, and alert you with an on-screen and/or audio signal when new mail arrives — hence the title of the movie *You've Got Mail*.)

This has revolutionized business operations, because now individuals working thousands of miles from each other can be in constant communication virtually free — with no long distance phone or fax charges necessary. (Our agency's offices in Ohio and Arizona stay online throughout the business day, with messages zipping among 20 or so workers whenever needed.)

Email is handy, of course, for shooting words and pictures and even audio and video files back and forth to one or more individuals. But an Internet site lets you "post" words and images that are accessible to anyone, at any time, without your being online. That's why it's called a "site."

To set up an Internet site, you simply reserve a place on the server of your ISP, where your words and pictures are stored.

You get an Internet address, where anybody can visit via their computer and modem, and see what you have stored there.

The Internet isn't just the World Wide Web, by the way. The well known "www" designation was established in 1993 in the process of taking the Internet out of the murky back rooms of scientists' laboratories and professors' studies and into the popular culture. But there are many Internet sites which don't include www in their addresses. (You don't need the www. for addresses like time.com or mindspring.com, for example.) And there will be fewer and fewer in years to come. Still, in casual conversation, there's little or no distinction between the "Internet," the "Net," the "World Wide Web," and the "Web." An Internet site *is* a website, and vice versa.

Internet site addresses always end in a special designation known as a "master domain." At the dawn of the Internet, addresses typically ended in .com to designate a company, .org to designate a nonprofit organization, .net to indicate a network, .edu for an educational institution, .gov referring to a government entity. Internet addresses based in other countries generally add a country code to the end, like .gt for Guatemala or .mk for the Former Yugoslav Republic of Macedonia.

Visit just about any Internet site and you'll find that it probably makes multiple "pages" of information available to you; so it's not quite as accurate to refer to a "Web page" or "home page." The home page , technically, is the first page that you find on your screen when you begin your visit to a site.

How can somebody in Argentina see *your* document on *their* computer screen? Furthermore, how can hundreds of people be looking at your Internet site simultaneously? On a website, everything is coded in a special computer language — usually HTML (hyper text markup language). One of the features of HTML is that it's "easy" — it will show off to anybody, as many as want to look.

So a number of visitors can be looking at your HTML-coded documents (which make up your website) simultaneously. Of course your server has to accommodate a lot of simultaneous visitors, and to do that, the server has arranged for a huge amount of "bandwidth" — the technological equivalent of a zillion incoming phone lines. Which is a lot of what you're paying for when you pay your ISP that monthly fee.

A "browser" isn't a guy in a clothing store who doesn't really plan to buy anything today. That's what a browser was in 1960. Today, a browser is a computer program that reads HTML (as well as some newer adjunct Internet languages like Java). The most common browsers in use at the turn of the millennium were Microsoft Internet Explorer and Netscape Navigator.

When you open your browser program, you have to

tell it where you want to go on the Internet. If you want to see a website, you type the address into the address line of the browser window. Normally you'll start with http:// — which translates roughly into "hypertext transfer protocol, here comes the address."

But browsers have already been so diligently and thoroughly refined by their designers that they do virtually everything for you — like adding the http:// to the beginning of the address if you don't. In fact, the latest editions of the major browsers will virtually "think" for you. If you type "servantheart" in the address line, for example, the browser figures you want to put http:// at the beginning, and maybe also www. — plus it adds a .com at the end of the address for good measure.

If it can't find an address like that, it will try other renditions of servantheart, like .org or .net ; and it will try the address without the www. at the beginning.

Furthermore, late-model browsers can "remember" the addresses you've visited, and as you begin to type an address, the browser will begin filling in additional letters that seem to match where you're headed.

There's much more you could learn about the Internet if you wanted — but the only other *essential* is this: Virtually every browser program includes a vital feature which should be used as often as needed. It's called "help." If you find yourself panicking, take a deep breath and click on it. There is probably some hope in there somewhere!

II.
FIVE SECRETS OF COMMUNICATION

🖙 SpeedLink:

This section is for YOU if ...

- You want to know **how donors decide** to become your donors
- You need to be convinced before you **invest** in a website for your ministry
- You feel that a website will **automatically solve** a lot of your ministry's problems
- You wonder how to **get people more interested** in what your ministry does
- You feel uneasy about how "clinical" and **impersonal** the Internet feels — and whether your donors will get the same feeling from your ministry
- You wonder how people will **locate** your ministry's website

---

Parlez-vous Internet?

Scriptural Secret #6:
· ·

God places a priority on quality communication, because it's a prerequisite to persuasion, conviction, response, and change.

Jesus went where the people were. He was sensitive to their customs. He spoke in the language of the people. And He brought tremendous change into their lives.

In **Matthew 9:35,36**, for example, we find that He "went through all the towns and villages, teaching in their synagogues, preaching the good news of the kingdom and healing every disease and sickness."

Galilee — a miserable backwater unappreciated by the upper classes — was never the same again. The work of Christ in that province was so significant that the Emperor Julian came to sneer at Jesus as "the Galileean God."

Clearly Jesus was communicating well. With Him, it wasn't just talk for talk's sake. He was driven by "compassion ... because they were harassed and helpless, like sheep without a shepherd."

If we feel the same compassion — if that's why we're in ministry in the first place, because we envision how people's lives can be better as a result of how God has called us to minister to them — then we will likewise find a way to go "through all the towns and villages, teaching in their synagogues, preaching the good news of the kingdom." And the language of the Internet is the ideal language for such a quest.

Some pooh-pooh the idea of ministry via the Internet because it seems to them like a prideful, ostentatious fad. ("Oh, everybody wants to be on the Internet these days!") But getting your ministry on the Internet is *not* just a matter of keeping up with the proverbial Joneses. It's a matter of being able to *communicate* with the Joneses — who are spending more and more time in cyberspace every month.

Without communication, ministry can't occur. In our book *The Seven Deadly Diseases of Ministry Marketing*, we started with a donor's gift and worked backward through the process that generated that gift. The "response" had to be preceded by "conviction" — the donor becoming *convinced* of the value of the proposition. Conviction had to be preceded by "persuasion" — the *process* of getting someone convinced. But how does persuasion occur? It happens by way of communication. The transmission of information from one party to another. ("How, then, can they call on the one they have not believed in?"

Romans 10:14 asks. "And how can they believe in the one of whom they have not heard? And how can they hear without someone preaching to them?")

Communication, however, can't happen in a vacuum. The speaker has to be engaged by the listener. Otherwise, all those words and pictures and ideas simply disperse into the atmosphere. When my nine-year-old daughter has her headphones on and the music cranked up, I can ask her to clean her room in English, pig Latin, and the original Greek if I want to — but she'll never budge. My speech about the merits of an orderly bedroom did not qualify as communication, because the speaker had not been engaged by the listener. Natalie, in fact, didn't qualify as a "listener" at all.

If my ministry produces great volumes of words, pictures, and ideas and funnels them all through conventional media (paper, broadcast, live events) — but a growing number of my target audience is spending a growing proportion of its life in front of a computer screen, surfing the Internet — I am a speaker without a listener! My God-given vision for helping people through my ministry is *dissipating* because I'm not going "through all the towns and villages" — finding the people where they are.

On the other hand, God has given us a fantastic gift in the form of HTML (our friend Matt Krepcho says it stands for "His Truth in Meaningful Language"), because this Internet language enables us to communicate with greater numbers of people *at a higher level of quality* than ever in human history. (And HTML's various cousins, including XML and others, will only increase the communication powers of the Internet.) As we are about to see, an Internet site is not simply an informational brochure posted on a computer screen. The Internet is *alive.* It has more capability for *involving* a person than television, radio, CDs, videos, or even *live events.*

Does this seem far-fetched? We'll see. Certainly there's not an overwhelming body of evidence available on the Internet at this time. Sadly, many ministry websites are badly designed, under-utilizing the amazing interactive communication capacity of the Internet.

But your ministry's website can be very different. The possibilities are thrilling. Through the Internet, you have the potential to speak to an individual *individually* (impossible in a sermon delivered to a sanctuary full of people), to get feedback from them *instantly* (impossible with TV, radio, or a response card tucked into a direct mail package), and to begin *immediately* tailoring all future communication with them to the feedback you've received (even telemarketing can't work that fast).

If such quality of communication seems like an impossible goal, that's a sign that we've lost sight of Christ's own standard. He spoke to individuals on their own terms, He got immediate feedback, and He tailored His approach accordingly. He talked to the woman at the well about living water. He talked to the heredity-conscious Nicodemus about a new birth.

The Internet lets us be more like Jesus in our communications than ever before.

Christians, caring about the world as Jesus did, and caring about fulfilling the ministries to which God has called them, should be the best communicators on the entire Internet.

Are we?

Let's go there.

Scriptural Secret #7:

Listening and the feedback that comes from it are every bit as valuable as talking and preaching. Giving the other person the opportunity to set their receptors to the ideal frequency, and then to speak their mind in response, is a manifestation of love. Love is practical.

The psalmist of the Scriptures urgently needed a conversation partner.

When he got in the deepest trouble, he wanted more than anything else for someone to *hear* him.

"*Hear* my voice in accordance with your *love*," he pleaded in **Psalm 119:149**; "preserve my life, O Lord...."

A God who wouldn't listen, wouldn't do him any good.

Over time, God's willingness to listen *defined* the psalmist's relationship with him.

"I love the Lord," he sang in **Psalm 116:1,2**, "for he *heard* my voice; he heard my cry for mercy. Because he turned his ear to me, I will call on him as long as I live.

In our work as Christian leaders, we tend to equate ministry with talking — teaching — telling. We tend to lose touch with the quality of God that most of the people in our target audience deeply long for. We have a God who *listens*. People want to be *heard*.

Which is perhaps the single most spectacular characteristic of the Internet.

Three features of an Internet site beautifully reflect the dynamic relationship between God and people:

1. Your website should be "interactive."

It's not just a string of letters and a series of images. It's not a brochure on your computer screen.

It has vitality. As a visitor, you can point the cursor on your computer screen to certain things, you can click your mouse or keyboard on them, and the website *responds* to that click as a *command*.

The implications for ministry and marketing are awesome. This means you can literally program your website to invite feedback and interaction from the visitor.

What was the single most important moment in the process of your coming to faith in Christ?

What is the most serious need facing America today?

Which of these potential projects would most accurately reflect your heart as a follower of Christ?

Which of these ministry products would mean the most to you?

Post your comments here about our latest book/video/event.

Click on any staff member's name to email that individual directly.

Would you take our survey? We'd love to get a "snapshot" of you! (Age, religious background, number of people in household, etc.)

There are innumerable questions you can ask visitors to your website. Your choice of questions will reflect the specific nature and mission of your ministry. In any case, the answers to these questions could prove to be worth tens of thousands of dollars in market research ... free!

Any feedback in the form of answers to multiple-choice questions can be easily stored in your own files, just like you store information about the donors you interact with via mail, phone, and events. You can "flag" a donor's record with his or her preferences — and communicate accordingly in the future.

But the Internet goes even further. A website can be programmed to "remember" a visitor, and use those learned details to tailor the way it communicates with that visitor in the future. For example, when I visit www.shockwave.com to get some fancy software, the site asks me my nickname. When I type in "Doug," the site responds with a screen that flies my name in like a Hollywood celebrity: "Doug, here's your Web Entertainment Center!"

Imagine someone visiting your ministry website, and finding that you address him or her by name: "Randy, we're glad you're here...." There's a strong feeling of belonging in that kind of exchange. The more opportunity you give a visitor to "personalize" your Internet site, the more connected he or she will feel to your ministry. (Check out www.hopenet.net for another example.)

2. Your website is easy to change.

You don't print 50,000 copies of your website and hope like crazy that there's no typo.

You "post" or "upload" your website — the actual posting normally takes only minutes — then revise it as often as you want. Daily, even hourly if you want to. Don't like the way that photograph ended up looking next to that headline? Replace it — in seconds — with a different photo. At no additional expense, other than the wage you're paying the person who actually clicks the keys to give the upload command.

Deciding on the content of your website, and designing the presentation of it, is an art — but posting it is a relatively simple science which can be accomplished by virtually any ministry staff member.

God's relationship with people is not static. He keeps communicating, keeps popping new experiences into our path.

It almost seems as if God were foreshadowing the Internet Age when he declared through Isaiah, "Forget the former things; do not dwell on the past" (**Isaiah 43:18**). Update your website frequently. Particularly if feedback from visitors tends to indicate one preference trend over another, steer your presentation in that direction. Don't change your mission — but keep the expression of your mission "up for grabs." (Andrew Brooks, CEO of Furniture.com — which sells *sofas* via the Internet! — used input provided by visitors to his website to redesign his site five times in eight months.)

If great things are happening in your ministry, get the word out by updating your site. "See, I am doing a new thing!" God proclaims in **Isaiah 43:19**. "Now it springs up; do you not perceive it?"

The typical visitor will check back in to your site within a month or so to see if you're offering anything new and interesting. If you don't have something fresh for visitors to experience, people won't keep coming back. The visitor who finds your site unchanged is likely never to return.

Got a new construction project underway? Post a new photo of the construction every day — scan a Polaroid! (Color scanners are getting as cheap as modems — some in the $100 range — and almost as simple to use.) Digital cameras (which allow you to skip the scanning process) are getting less and less expensive all the time. You can easily link a digital camera to a website so that an updated shot is automatically posted every 60 seconds! In any case, posting *any* kind of photo update is visible evidence of how people's donations are being put to work.

Starting a new outreach campaign? Run a photo of the

person who inspired it — or an individual who represents the type of person who will be helped by it. Post a new testimony every week; show the results of your ministry! Run a quotation by that individual. You can even post a video or audio clip, so if I'm visiting your site and I want to see or hear it for myself, I can access the experience with the click of my mouse.

Did you reach a big goal? Post the news on your site. Run a photo of the victory celebration. Or a photo of whatever you were able to acquire or change or do by reaching the goal.

Whatever constitutes the latest news in your ministry ... put it on your website!

3. Like it or not, the visitor controls some of the experience.

One of the most fascinating facets of the Christian faith is how relentlessly God protects our *freedom*. We are always free to listen to Him or not. Sure, we suffer the consequences for busting His design and going our own way; but even so, He never forces us to do what's right. God chooses to be the Master who serves.

In a way, the Internet obeys the same principle. The individual visiting your website has the power to decide the width of your columns of type, how much of your text and graphics fit on the screen, how much of his computer screen is occupied by your message, and so forth. In fact, if your website isn't programmed to "lock in" the details, the visitor could actually decide (or his browser will decide by default) what fonts your website appears in, how big the type is, what color it appears in, and so on.

Which means the design of your Internet site must account for a number of variations which don't exist in the world of print or broadcast. Many ministry marketers have spent years working to *control* the impressions made on donors. In a direct mail letter format package, for example, the marketer dictates the colors, the size of the paper, the sizes of the type, even to an extent the *sequence* in which the donor will read the various components in the package (there's a whole sub-science to the matter of "insertion order" in direct mail). I've even been known to obsess about mid-sentence page breaks in order to encourage the reader to turn the page. In direct mail, then, the marketer is largely in charge. The poor reader only gets to decide whether to read or not, and how much to read before deciding how or whether to respond.

But control freaks freak out when they get to marketing on the Internet. The old standards of imposing an experience on the donor don't apply as strictly anymore. The visual realm is much more fluid.

As a consequence, the *message* of a website must be that much more compelling. What does your ministry actually *do*? How can you actually *benefit* me? What are you really *accomplishing*? Why should I want to get involved? On the Internet, the old substance-vs.-style seesaw now tilts dramatically. Now that someone else is deciding many issues of style, we as ministry marketers have to provide real substance — or find ourselves dangling on the up-end of the teeter-totter.

Scriptural Secret #8:

Even though God pursues people rather than waiting for them to pursue Him, He reaches out to them *through us*. It's not automatic ("How can they believe in the one of whom they have not heard?" — Romans 10:14); we have to get the word out.

Paul asked the Christians at Colosse for prayer. Pray "that God may open a door for our message," he urged them in **Colossians 4:3,4**, "so that we may proclaim the mystery of Christ.... Pray that I may proclaim it clearly, as I should."

An open door was a sensible prayer target for Paul; he was probably in jail when he wrote these words. But his objective wasn't just to get an open door. He always added a "so that": He wanted the open door "so that" he could "proclaim the mystery of Christ," and "clearly."

He was striving to live out Christ's Great Commission of **Mark 16:15**: "Go into all the world and preach the good news to all creation." In fact, Paul goes on to say in **Colossians 4:5**, "Be wise in the way you act toward outsiders; make the most of every opportunity." We must make the most of every evangelistic opportunity!

Our calling is not a sit-back-and-watch kind of calling. It is a get-up-and-do kind of calling, a "Go ye" calling.

With the Internet, Paul could have reached the world from his prison cell! But he didn't have the Internet; we do. We have the open door! The chains are off, the shackles are broken. We can reach a planet full of people — or we *will* be able to, in a tick or two of the cosmic clock.

But will we proclaim Christ, and clearly? Will we get up and "go" to the world? Maybe; maybe not. (The great problem of the gospel hasn't been that the lost won't come — but rather that the saved won't go.)

One of the most common pitfalls of ministries on the Internet is their strategy of posting a website and then not telling anyone it's there.

We want to believe that people are eagerly searching for exactly the kind of ministry our organization offers. But in fact, only a tiny percentage of people are proactively interested in finding us. The rest must have their lives *interrupted* by the news that we're here and available to help. Even those who *might* be interested in us need to be given *every possible encouragement* to find us — and *conveniently*.

In terms of the Internet, this translates into a number of practical strategies. First, we need to ask ourselves exactly *how* people using the Internet go about the challenge of finding anything on it. How do people actually "surf" the Net?

There are four answers to this question.

1. People surf the Net by *search engine.*

Almost as quickly as the Internet was born, search engines (and their first cousin, Internet directories) were born. These are websites themselves, but their purpose is to help people find stuff on the Internet. You go to a certain search engine site — say, HotBot (www.hotbot.com) or the directory known as Yahoo (www.yahoo.com) — and the site gives you an opportunity to search the Net by way of key words.

How does HotBot, for example, know that there are 54,680 pages on the Internet that include both the word

Christian and the word *money*? The geniuses at HotBot have rigged a computer program to be their "robot" — or "bot," in the slang of the Internet. This bot sends a "spider" out to "crawl" across the World Wide Web. The spider's function? It searches, continually, through an interminable string of possible Internet addresses, in hopes of finding something new. When it does, it adds that entry to its memory files. When I go to www.hotbot.com and type in the words *Christian* and *money*, the super-powerful HotBot server scans its memory files and reports within a few seconds that it has, to date, found exactly 54,680 pages which include *both* words. The power and speed of HotBot's computers is what makes it such a valuable search engine; I don't have to wait even five seconds for the answer to my question. HotBot also gives me the option of searching for Internet sites which include exact multi-word phrases — like *Christian money*, in that order.

When HotBot was launched in 1995, its founders bragged that it could canvas the entire Internet every 90 days. Since then the Net has grown so huge that HotBot now covers only an estimated 17% of it!

So the major search engines are searching the Net continuously, looking for that brand-new site your ministry has just posted. But as the Internet grows, this process takes longer and longer. You might post your site today, and find that HotBot hasn't discovered it even three weeks from now — or three months from now — or longer.

You don't have to wait. And you shouldn't. You can *register* with search engines and directories. You can *tell* them that you're on the Internet, give them your Web address, and ask them to add you to their files. Some search engines are free; some charge small fees.

Of course, there are now search engines that do

nothing but search for new *search engines* — so it's probably best to find someone who makes it their business to register new Internet sites on all the most productive search engines. (Our agency provides this service to client-ministries. When we get involved in Internet development with any ministry, we build in the immediate registration of the ministry's website with up to 200 *search engines.*)

But when I ask HotBot for all the Internet sites that include the words *Christian* and *money*, it gives me a long list. A list 54,680 names long. (Actually HotBot will only give me a maximum of 100 addresses at a time; then I have to demand the next 100 by clicking a "more" button. Obviously I'm likelier to select a site in the first dozen or so choices than, say, #22,471 on the list. How does HotBot, or any search engine, decide in what *sequence* to display addresses? Earlier positions, then, have greater value.

Search engines typically keep secret the "formula" they use for deciding sequence, but we do know that it happens not only on the basis of the words appearing on the first page of a site, but also on the basis of "meta tags." These are bits of code built into the site — but invisible on the screen — which catch the eye of any passing "spiders." Meta tags are comprised of key words that relate to that specific website. Our agency's www.berkeybrendelsheline.com website, for example, doesn't include the word "money" on the first page of the site. But we wanted to show up on search engine listings for anyone interested in raising *money* for their ministry, so we built in an invisible meta tag with the key word *money*. When you register your site with a search engine, they'll also ask you to supply 20 or more key words which they attach to their listing of your Web address — so you'll show up on more searches. The challenge is to choose the most effective key words,

words which connect to your unique ministry.

2. People surf the Net by *typing "guess" words.*

In the address window of your browser application, you would expect to type a long, relatively complicated Web address like http://www.bookofhope.com. But in the most recent versions of the major browsers, you can simply type in the main word of the address — in this case, bookofhope — and the browser automatically adds the necessary details before and after. In a split second, it not only adds http:// but also checks to see if www. is necessary; and it goes through the likeliest suffixes, starting with .com and .net , then moving to the less frequently used ones. Only if it can't figure out what you're guessing at will it throw itself back on your mercy. (Hm, where would I find Berkey Brendel Sheline? I type in "berkeybrendelsheline," and almost instantly find myself at www.berkeybrendelsheline.com — even though we also maintain our "sentimental" domain name, www.servantheart.com, which leads visitors to the same site.)

All of which means it usually makes the most sense to choose an address for your site which is based on a key word likely to be "guessed at" by the most surfers. Type in "time" and you'll go to Time magazine's website http://www.time.com. Type "sportsillustrated" and you go to the CNN/Sports Illustrated site.

3. People surf the Net by *linking.*

This is, in fact, probably the most common means by which anybody finds any Internet site. A person is at a certain website, there's a link to another website, they click on it, and they go there.

If there's a directory of ministries, for example,

related to your type of ministry, email the directory and ask to have your Web address included as a link.

At our agency's website, www.berkeybrendelsheline.com, we list our current clients, with links to their websites whenever available. Visit our website, and you can go directly to *their* website. That's the process that gave birth to the term *surfing*. You're moving back and forth across the water, catching whatever next wave strikes your fancy.

4. People surf the Net by *direction*.

In other words, they do what you tell them to do. You advertise your Web address, and some will deliberately type it into their browsers and visit your site.

The reality is that a ministry must feature its Internet site address in absolutely every possible medium, every possible situation, every possible opportunity. Include it as religiously as you include your name and logo, your address and phone. Put it on response devices in mailings, on letterhead (including envelopes and business cards), on brochures, in radio and TV spots, in print advertisements, even in telemarketing, and on public signage. **You have an Internet site? Good. But nobody knows it. You've got to shout it from the proverbial housetops. Drive people to your site by every available means.**

Promote your Internet site especially to your current donors, as a means of intensifying their relationship with your ministry. Cross-pollination is crucial to your marketing strategy. Promote your Internet address to your radio audience, for example, in the same way you would promote your radio program through a direct mail package.

By the way, don't include http:// when you feature your address — that part of the address is a "given," and it looks amateurish to include it; just start with www. (or the main word, if you don't use www.). And because of the unique endings of Internet addresses, you don't even need to specify "Internet" or "World Wide Web" —simply *show* the address, and let it speak for itself; people will know that anything ending in .com , .net , .org , or the like is an Internet address.

(And while you're promoting your Internet address, particularly in direct response packages, **ask the donor for his or her email address**. Include a request for email address just as consistently as you request a street address. The day will soon come when a major portion of your donor communications can occur via email — at a breathtakingly reduced cost to your ministry!)

However, simply showing your Web address isn't as compelling as specific, targeted promotion. **The more specific your pitch is — "Visit our website to see the latest on our progress on XYZ effort" — the likelier you'll be to get visitors.** This takes far more effort, but it results in far greater impact.

Driving people to your website will become more and more crucial as the Internet continues to expand. There are already millions of sites on the Internet. Competition for visitors is fierce, and getting more so. In fact, as people become overwhelmed by the vast array of available information, they are relying more and more on "portals" — websites which organize Web addresses into interest groups, often tailored to the individual's stated preferences. A portal essentially tells someone what's important and what's not. If you surf the Net and find a

....

portal that seems to be designed for people likely to take an interest in your ministry, contact the portal and find out how much it will cost to be listed on their site.

The growing presence of portals on the Internet is simply one more major piece of evidence for the fact that you must drive people to your site; you cannot simply build it and expect them to come. It is critical that we grasp this truth and act on it, because more and more people today are using the Internet like we used to use the phone book: to find goods, services, and information.

(If they're moving to a new town, they look for a new church on the Net. The church where I serve as a teaching pastor — Mountain Valley Church in Scottsdale, Arizona — was born in 1993 thanks to intensive direct mail campaigns; I called it "the church that junk mail built." But with the growth of traffic on our website, www.lifechange.org, it's fast becoming "the church that the Internet built." Growing numbers of new attenders are coming in through the Internet door instead of the direct mail door.)

And because more and more people are online all day long, it's more and more *convenient* for people to use the Internet like a phone book . It's not as complicated as booting up your computer (it's probably on all day already), "logging on" to the Internet (if you're online already and staying online), and launching a browser application (many computers can launch a browser in a second or two; many are powerful enough to leave multiple applications active simultaneously, so a browser can always be available). It's not even as complicated as finding a phone number in a phone book, because of the many search engines and directories on the Net.

Furthermore, **people don't surf the Net to find a phone number and then pick up the phone and call**

— because the Internet makes it possible to jump there almost instantly, simply by clicking on a "link." In a second or two, they've gone to *see* the website of the party they've located. They "visit" the church by browsing through the church's website. They "meet" your ministry by browsing through your ministry's website. (In virtual 3-D showrooms at commercial sites, customers are actually moving furniture around in model living rooms, or trying clothes on various body types, or taking animated tours, according to R.R. Donnelley's Peggy Pulliam.) Visitors to a website can interact with your ministry, providing feedback — and even give on the spot. But the church or ministry that hasn't spread the word about its website *loses out* on a prospective new relationship!

Do not build a website and then hide it. "No one lights a lamp and hides it in a jar or puts it under a bed," Jesus pointed out in **Luke 8:16**. "Instead, he puts it on a stand, so that those who come in can see the light."

Put your website on a stand. Shine the light!

Missing Persons

Scriptural Secret #9:
....

God cares more about people than He does about programs, institutions, trends, or even religions.

The most under-used Internet technique in the entire world of charitable ministries is the technique of people telling their own stories.

The most powerful, proven technique of raising money for Christian charities is the technique of telling the true story of a *life changed by the power of God's love through that ministry*.

Real-life *results* make a far greater impact on a prospective donor than any amount of information about a ministry's procedures or programs.

This is no accident. It reflects God's design of our world — and His design reflects His heart. He loves people — He "so loved the world that he gave his one and only Son" (**John 3:16**). Theoretically, any Christian ministry exists to change people's lives, to help people. Sadly, however, hundreds of charities post websites and *never tell a single story* — never let me meet a single individual whose life is different today because of that ministry.

Yet the Internet is the *perfect* venue for sharing that kind of high-impact information. You can post a photograph of a person, with the text of their story adjacent to it. It's an easy matter to make that text scroll for easy reading. Or offer an audio clip of that person telling his or her own story, or a part of it. It's compelling to see a person's face and actually hear them speaking out loud! You can easily animate the person's face, programming your website to move automatically through a series of photographic images of the person. Or offer a video clip, so I can see and hear the person movie-style. None of this happens as effectively on paper, in a letter package or brochure or book. Even switching from black-and-white to color photos in a direct mail package can be an expensive proposition — but full color on the Internet is *free*!

And the simplicity of posting images and text on the Internet also allows you to rotate your stories frequently, so visitors don't get the same old story every time they stop by.

The power of the true story of an individual whose life has been changed is so significant — and this so frequently proves to be the most effective possible technique for raising ministry money — that our agency team uses the abbreviation **SOTO: Story Of The One**. The single best means of communicating what your ministry is accomplishing is *not* to chart out your organizational structure, or map out your project procedures, or produce a grid full of figures. The single best means of communicating what your ministry is accomplishing is to tell me the SOTO, the story of "the one." Tell me who they were, how they were struggling, how they crossed your path, what your ministry did, and how it turned out. God planted His love of people in our hearts. We instinctively want to learn about people. This is God's design of our human nature — and the Internet isn't going to change that!

In some 20 years of working with Christian ministries, we observe that some ministry leaders tend to be emotional, and fail to give donors enough hard information on which to base a giving decision. Other ministry leaders tend to be clinical, and fail to express themselves with enough passion to capture the imagination of donors. We sympathize with both varieties — and offer the SOTO as the perfect solution. **The true story of a life touched and transformed by the power of God's love through your ministry provides *actual evidence* of your ministry's validity for the individual who needs more information than your leader is naturally inclined to give. Meanwhile, the same story can provide the *heart-touch* that is sorely lacking in a more business-like leader's natural style of communication.**

If you don't have an apparatus for collecting such true stories, set one up. Almost no investment can be more important. Provide simple tell-me-a-story forms to the people who do your work in the field; email your entire staff once a quarter and ask them to feed back stories to you; ask donors on the back of direct mail reply devices to share their stories; solicit true stories via your website itself!

If your ministry is really touching lives, tell the world! No news will go further toward turning a "prospect" into a donor, or a "casual" donor into a "committed" one.

Scriptural Secret #10:

God is no respecter of demographics. He loves everybody the same. But Jesus spoke to people as unique individuals, and won them over on that basis. He has given us, in the Internet, an opportunity to reach a wider variety of people "types" — yet speak to each in his or her own language.

Jesus unnerved Nathanael in **John 1:47,48**, when he revealed that he had been watching him secretly. In a phrase or two, Jesus had identified him as a thoroughly honest man, yet with somewhat limited spiritual vision. That encounter wedded Nathanael to Jesus, and he became one of the Nazarene's 12 closest friends.

Jesus and the Samaritan woman of **John 4** spoke the same language but had a cross-cultural dialogue. "Come, see a man who told me *everything* I *ever did*," she exclaimed in **John 4:29**. "Could this be the Christ?"

Jesus had supernatural powers of observation, and He used these powers beautifully in connecting with people. We have very limited powers of observation by comparison, and even the powers we *do* have often go sadly under-used. But the Internet gives us unprecedented opportunities for observing people and connecting with them on the basis of those observations.

If I had some way of knowing details about each individual donor to my ministry — what part of our ministry appeals to her the most, how she prefers to be addressed, what kinds of information she finds superfluous or annoying — I still wouldn't be able to redesign a direct mail appeal letter package, for example, uniquely for each donor. At the very most, I can collect data about donors' preferences and segment the file in broad terms, targeting versions of mailings to each segment.

The Internet, on the other hand, enables us to $\boxed{\text{ask}}$ a visitor his or her preferences, $\boxed{\text{record}}$ those preferences automatically, and $\boxed{\text{communicate}}$ with that individual $\boxed{\textbf{according to}}$ those preferences. Sun Microsystems, for example (at www.sun.com), enables the visitor to click on "MySun" and personalize the types of information that will appear on the screen every time he visits the site. Want information about new graphics software? Choose accordingly — and graphic software news appears up front every time you visit MySun. MySun goes so far as to let you specify the *layout* of the information on the screen, not to mention the nickname you want to be called (which appears in a friendly little greeting at the top of the page). USWest lets its email users (at www.uswestmail.net) choose to read in English or Spanish, and thousands of websites offer even more varied language choices.

Even if you don't go to the trouble of creating a personalized Web page, you can include a $\boxed{\text{survey}}$ in your website — and communicate with the individual on the basis of those answers, either by email or (more clumsily) via mail or phone. **Ask the visitor what information they'd like to receive — let them choose from among the many and varied aspects of your ministry. You can follow up with a periodical $\boxed{\textbf{"e-zine"}}$ — an emailed newsletter. It doesn't have to be complicated to fulfill the visitor's wishes: Include all the same features in everybody's e-zine, but re-arrange the order so that the individual's favorite topic is addressed first.**

The Internet handily enables us to escape the twin traps of "distinct-ness" and "identified-ness." These are "illnesses" from which many ministry marketers suffer. Those who are *distinct* have the idea that donors are utterly unlike them; those who are *identified* feel that donors are *completely* like them. Both views tend to color the way a ministry communicates with donors and prospects. The distinct marketer tends to over-inform (or over-emote) in order to persuade the individual to give. The identified marketer tends to under-inform — or share too much essentially boring detail about how the ministry is run — because the donor is assumed to be of the same mind as the people who work inside the ministry. But a website has the capacity to derive the *truth* about the visitor's mindset and communicate accordingly — enabling you to present the aspects of your ministry that will relate most successfully to the visitor. Relating to the visitor is the key!

We naturally wish we could nail down the whole audience in one big clump and communicate to that profile. Our tendency is to ask, "What are the *general* demographics of Internet users?" Certainly much has been written about the general demographics of Internet users — how they're not the typical older female donors that most Christian ministries rely on. Typically, the Internet is being accessed by young, wealthy, and well educated people — and a larger proportion of males than in the traditional ministry donor base. Younger donors — imagine! For many ministries, a younger donor base would be a shock to the system. And these people are more comfortable shopping and searching for information online, and donating via credit card online. (As long ago as 1996, Rainforest Action Network found that the new members it signed up online — or signed up by traditional mail after an individual's initial visit to the website — tended to be *better donors*, according to *MicroTimes*.)

But beware: Even the prevailing demographic of the

typical Internet user is changing as more people get online. Eventually, the Internet population will reflect the general population — and perhaps sooner than we think. My personal bias is that an older individual may take longer to get online in the first place, but then will spend more time online — at least from home — than someone at the height of a career. My parents, for example, only got online after my brother and I bought them Web TV. But now, with Mom retired and Dad working four days a week, they're online at home as much as 12 hours a week — and buying stuff left and right!

It would be a shame to post your ministry's website with just one generic type of visitor in mind, not taking advantage of the Internet's fabulous ability to speak to individual preferences. Jesus talked to everybody, but He talked to every individual. He spoke to Jews and Samaritans alike. In fact, He went out of His way to do so. **Acts 1:8** tells us that Christ's last command should be our first concern! The Internet makes it more possible than ever. This, indeed, may be the closest we will ever get to experiencing the thrill of what Jesus had — supernatural powers of observation, and the satisfaction of using those powers to connect personally and meaningful with the people God loves.

III.
FIVE SECRETS OF RELATIONSHIP

≡**☞ SpeedLink:**

This section is for YOU if ...

- The **leaders** of your ministry aren't really interested in the Internet
- Your ministry team members **disagree** about what your website should emphasize
- You can't decide whether to focus your website on getting **new donors** or dealing with existing donors
- You want practical, plain-English **ideas** for how to design your website
- You wonder how you'll be able to tell whether your website is actually **"working"**

The More You Pay, the More It's Worth

Scriptural Secret #11:

Whatever you value, you invest in; whatever you invest in pays dividends. Whatever you don't invest in won't pay dividends. If you're not investing in it, you don't value it — regardless of how strongly you insist otherwise.

We like the first part of **Luke 6:38**, where Jesus said, "Give, and it will be given to you. A good measure, pressed down, shaken together and running over, will be poured into your lap."

That sounds fine!

But before we even get out of the verse, Jesus has inserted a reality check: "For with the measure you use, it will be measured to you."

We might say Jesus was a realist. He understood thoroughly how God had designed the world, and the truths He taught us were based on the sheer practicalities of that system. Sure, you get a return on investment. But use a teaspoon to pour in, and a teaspoon-trickle comes back out. Use a dump truck up front, and your return shows up in truckloads. The apostle Paul observed the same principle, and put it plainly in **2 Corinthians 9:6**: "Whoever sows sparingly will also reap sparingly, and whoever sows generously will also reap generously."

All of which applies to our ministries — and no less so in the area of Internet communications.

We observe many ministry leaders offering something of a nod, and little more, to the importance of the Internet. Without strong backing from the front office, the staff members responsible for posting a website often find themselves under-resourced. The resulting site is spare, perhaps static, and typically stale, with little or no attention to updates. In such scenarios, it's not uncommon to hear the ministry leader or senior staff observe that "the Internet isn't working for us."

The Internet is not magic. It takes work; it requires attention and investment. People can't just sit in church an hour a week and *hear* the Word, but have to go out and *do* it day by day in order for the Word to produce fruit in their lives. Likewise, you can't just read theory about the Internet, or even post a lame website, and somehow hope that your ministry will be deluged with new donors.

While our agency has been blessed with a number of Web-savvy clients, it is generally rare to find a ministry leader who is knowledgeable about the Internet. This is perhaps as it should be. Most ministry leaders have jam-packed schedules; if they're spending hours a day camped out online, something's wrong. A TV preacher doesn't have to be a video technology wizard. But a ministry's Internet outreach has to be regarded as important — and supported accordingly — or it will not *become* important as a revenue source for the ministry.

So a ministry leader with little or no understanding of the Internet needs to get an education — or truly empower a trusted staff member to make the ministry's Internet outreach happen. If a ministry leader commits to spending just one hour a week surfing the Net, the education will be invaluable — and a stream of ideas for harnessing the power of the Net for the ministry will likely begin flowing.

How important do the leaders of your ministry consider your ministry's website? The answer to that question will manifest itself in the quality of your site, the attention it is given by staff, and the impact it makes on visitors.

There are dozens of reasons for a ministry to postpone posting a website, or lag behind in updating the site they've posted. But none of these reasons overrides the fact that a stale, static site — or no site at all — fails to build relationships with donors the way a fresh, zippy site could. **It is true in marriage and ministry and marketing alike: True relationship occurs because of what you *do*, not what you say or think or hope.**

A ministry's commitment to establishing and building donor relationships via the Internet is often most keenly expressed in a seemingly insignificant routine: *how quickly a visitor's email is answered.* A good website gives the visitor an opportunity to type a note to someone inside the ministry operation; but in many cases these emails funnel indiscriminately to a "webmaster" — the person who physically maintains the website (often a vendor, not even a staff member). The webmaster may forward emails to the appropriate staff member, but on what priority basis?

Internet users tend to expect prompt feedback, simply because email is perceived as "instant communication." It's unrealistic, of course, to email a ministry in the middle of the night and expect a staff person to offer an intelligent response — or any response at all — before the next workday. But Net surfers have no real incentive to be realistic; they are living and functioning in the world of their perceptions (just like all of us).

Commercial businesses have learned the hard way that "customer expectations are raised" by using the Internet, as they expect online orders to be filled faster, according to Fred Goss in the May 1999 issue of *What's Working*. "This is an irrational expectation since ... the process of fulfilling an order is exactly the same however the order is received." But it happens anyway!

It's a simple matter to set up an "auto-respond" message which goes automatically and instantly to anyone emailing you via your website. This message can thank them for the contact and let them know that their email is being routed to the appropriate staff member (if they requested some kind of feedback). If possible, commit to getting a personal response back to them within a certain number of days — one work day, if possible. (You can also use the auto-response to promote an upcoming project or event, or make a free offer.)

Whatever you tell the visitor, make sure it's the truth — as perceived by the visitor. Goss tells of seeing an ad in a hockey magazine for a catalog he was interested in. The web address was featured in the ad, so he went online to request it — and got an instant auto-response promising to mail him the catalog within "a few days." He got it two weeks later. Even though they had told him the truth technically — if they waited a few days, then mailed it by some cheap rate, it would take two weeks total to receive the catalog — it *felt* like a dropped ball. Better to say something along the lines of "We'll get you your catalog within a couple weeks."

It's also a good idea, Goss points out, to note your ministry's telephone number adjacent to the email link, so a person who doesn't want to wait for an email exchange can make contact by phone.

The famous folks at Amazon.com, who started out selling books but now sell and auction way more than just books, have mastered the art of online customer relations. J. Neil Weintraut and Jeffrey Davis, writing in the July 1999 issue of *Business* 2.0, say Amazon's focus isn't on selling books, but "customer ecstasy." Visit www.amazon.com for the first time, place an order, and you'll experience it personally. First you have the opportunity to create a super-fast "one-click" ordering setup for yourself. When you place an order, you get auto-email confirmation that your order has been received *and* a day or two later when your order has been *shipped*. Even if you change a detail of your account record, like your email address, you get instant notification at both the old and new email addresses:

Hi,

The e-mail address on your account with amazon.com has been changed.

The old address was brendel@servantheart.com.

The new address is amazon@dougbrendel.com.

We just thought you would want to be informed — just in case it wasn't you who changed it!

Amazon.com Customer Service

The feeling you get is that Amazon *loves* you, *cares* about you, and is *tracking* with you and *taking care of you!* Yet everything they're doing is *automated*. The secret is that the leaders have thought through how to *use* the available technology to *communicate* care to the customer. Ministries would do well to follow Amazon's model.

(Okay, one more excellent detail about doing business with Amazon — more evidence of their commitment to "customer ecstasy," although not related to technology: When you get your order, there's a freebie in the package, completely unannounced — a classy little notepad, with a small, dignified rendering of the Amazon logo unobtrusively situated at the top. This is the kind of touch that endears Amazon to its customers. How many ministries add a classy bonus product of high perceived value when they ship anything to a donor? We often insert additional *promotional* materials, but an item of greater perceived value to the *donor* than to the *ministry* will make a far more positive emotional impact on the donor.)

The idea of "investing" in donors is received with a shiver by many ministries. There's a tendency to think only in terms of wanting the *donor* to invest in *us*. But in fact, the principle of Luke 6:38 — "Give, and it will be given to you" — applies very specifically to our relationships with donors. The Internet tests our commitment to investing in donors and prospective donors. One of the hottest single words in all of cyberspace is "free." Offer something for free, and you have an audience. Give something away, no strings attached, and you generate interest.

But offering something free is a foreign concept to many ministries. We've learned to dislike the "feeling" of offering something for free, as if it constitutes a "baiting" of the donor. Jesus, however, offered salvation free of charge to whoever believes (**John 3:16**), no strings attached — with the promise of new life (**John 10:10**), as His Spirit began nudging the new believer into a life based on God's design. Twenty centuries of organized religion taught people the opposite concept: that you have to "be good" and earn your salvation. That same distortion of God's grace infects the marketing of our ministries. We're reluctant to offer something free, for fear it will be seen as bait — as if becoming involved in our ministry will be *unhealthy* for the donor. **The fact is, giving is a healthy part of the life — it's part of God's design for us — and it will do *spiritual good for the donor* to become involved in supporting our ministry financially!** So we should be eager to get people involved by just about whatever means we can. If offering something of value free of charge via the Internet will attract new donors, let's do it. (The key is to control costs — not to make every individual function or strategy pay for itself instantly.)

The apostle Paul recognized that he had a right to compel Christians to support his work financially, but he didn't want to exercise that right. "What then is my reward?" he asks in a discussion of the topic in **1 Corinthians 9**. "Just this: that in preaching the gospel I may offer it free of charge...." He was much more satisfied to give his ministry away, and inspire believers to engage in financial support as they came to see the value of what he was doing.

Our agency strongly recommends offering **something valuable** (though not necessarily expensive) *free of charge* **on the very first page of a ministry's website**. (Go to our site at www.berkeybrendelsheline.com, for example, and you can download a chapter of *Seven Deadly Diseases of Ministry Marketing* instantly. Offering a chapter for free, not the whole book, actually promotes purchase of the book.) **The chances of motivating**

longer-term involvement with your ministry go up dramatically among people who have received something of value from you without charge. Commercial business has already discovered this. Fred Goss observes in the May 31, 1999, issue of *What's Working*, "If you can get them to the website — and [they] take your freebie, one in three will buy."

One superb free offer is a ministry "e-zine" — or electronic newsletter. Assuming your ministry now publishes and mails a "traditional" newsletter, adapt the articles for the Internet so they can be easily emailed and read online. Offer a free subscription to your ministry's e-zine on the first page of your website, and you not only endear yourself to the visitor, but you capture his or her email address — and gain the opportunity of communicating about your ministry to that person on a regular basis.

You can think of an e-zine as a commercial for your website. Excerpts or condensations of the website articles appear in the e-zine, along with links which allow the reader to click and go directly to the full piece at the website. Ideally, you'll have a triangle — your newsletter, your website, and your e-zine. The e-zine arrives on my computer screen, it makes me want to read more at the website, I click on the link and go to the site (more text and more pictures than the e-zine), I read the longer version, then the newsletter arrives in the mail and gives me more detail still.

E-zines will likely grow in value to ministries over the next few years. "Even if deleted before read," Gary Grant said in a 1999 speech entitled *Using the Internet in Fundraising*, "such a piece can make people **feel more connected** and **more likely to support** than the organization they only hear from once or twice a year (and then only for money)."

What else could you offer for free?

You could offer email updates — simple, straightforward news tidbits about advances your ministry is making on any effort, project, or campaign. It's not too glamorous, but someone interested in what your ministry is doing might go for it. This could be as simple as saying on the first page of your site, "I would love to be able to email you and let you know about new stuff on our site that could help you. Would you let me?"

You could offer a screen-saver — that graphic file which replaces the background of your computer screen. These are completely emailable.

You could find any number of products related to your ministry, stockpile a quantity of them at an acceptable cost to you, and consider the expense a valid investment in the generation of new donors.

Or give away a devotional — either downloadable (totally a benefit to the visitor, not as much to the ministry, since you don't capture the visitor's street or email address) or emailable (a lesser perceived benefit to the donor, since they have to request it — although you can set up the devotional as an auto-response which comes to them instantly — but a greater benefit to the ministry since you capture the email address). You can also offer a free instant product via email but with the initial requirement of a street address — a rather obvious ploy to capture the mailing address.

You may wish to offer a Bible reading schedule — one of the read-through-the-Bible-in-a-year variety, or perhaps one uniquely designed for your ministry, with an emphasis on passages related to your mission.

Or offer weekly, bi-weekly, or monthly encouragements — even a daily schedule is doable because of automation technology.

Or offer to email a "Scripture of the day."

Or offer articles on spiritual-growth subjects.

Or offer any of an infinite variety of other beneficial

products to your website visitors (any of which our agency can help you develop).

The Internet, in any case, gives you the opportunity to **test** **the effectiveness of any offer in a relatively short time span**. Keep in mind, however, that offering something downloadable (like our sample chapter) doesn't capture the visitor's email address. Offering something emailable (like an e-zine) doesn't capture the visitor's street address. Only offering something which must be *mailed* will capture the visitor's street address — and while most ministries generate primary revenues through direct mail, the street address may be essential to your marketing operation. Each level of investment, in other words, relates to a different level of potential return.

Scriptural Secret #12:

Money follows ministry, not the other way around. And ministry is relationship. Focus on relationship, God will enable ministry, and money can follow. Relationship is the key. People reward it; God values it.

What should your ministry's website actually look like? What should it say, what should it do?

Perhaps the most important model to guide the design of your ministry's website is the model of Christ's character. If our churches and ministries are what they ought to be, they will be Christlike in character — and the qualities of Christ's character will be expressed in our websites too.

Some don't understand that a website needs to reflect the organization behind it; they think of a website as existing in a totally different universe. To be sure, some aspects of Internet presentation are unique to the Internet — but by and large, when someone arrives at your website, it should be the "virtual you." Your site will make an impression; it should reflect your church or ministry's character and personality. A current member or donor will automatically compare his or her existing impression of your church or ministry to the impression that your website makes, and there will either be good alignment or a disconnect.

Practically speaking, Christ majored on building His Father's kingdom through relationships — and so should our websites. (Those of us whose ministries don't really major on relationships will soon be exposed by the failure of our websites.) An emphasis on relationships translates into a key strategic decision in the design of your site: **Focus on getting qualified new names on your mailing list rather than trying to raise money directly.**

Does this disappoint you? It disappoints me. I want there to be a secret formula for turning your website into a cash cow. But the fact is, no such formula exists. Perhaps God ordained that the Internet would function in this way for the sake of our spiritual health. He requires to see us focus on relationships first, and let resources follow according to His design. As Matt Krepcho says, "God promised to 'feed the birds,' but He doesn't throw bird seed into the nest. Money will follow ministry, but not automatically. God could drop millions of dollars into each ministry's bank account. But I'm convinced that if He took away our need to fund-raise, we wouldn't *deal* with people; we would only handle *projects!*"

Of course, a new name on your mailing list must be "converted" to donor status, and that conversion process takes time and money. Even major media ministries have found that the "conversion rate" of donors who first respond via a prime-time TV special can be very different from that of donors who first respond via a mailing or a magazine ad.

If you focus your website primarily on acquiring new names, will they convert? Will they cost an arm and a leg to convert? Will you have to mail them a dozen letters and plead with them on the phone for that first donation? Actually, our agency's experience has been that the character of Christ — relationship over resources — is pretty faithfully reflected in Internet donor relations. **Conversion of new, qualified Internet-acquired names to donor status appears to be working well.** We test as often as our ministry clients will allow; and in a recent 5,000-person test we conducted, we got a higher than average gift amount and higher than average percentage of response.

This kind of information may encourage us to think of our websites as devices **not for "getting donations," but for *making friends***. It's passé, after all, to think of the Internet as cold and clinical. Because of the potential for technology to replicate human interaction, the Net represents an opportunity for a keener sense of community, the building of "family," and relationship with ministry partners than ever since the industrialization of society. (Before that, when there was no mechanization, people were more or less stuck together. "Community" was imposed on them!) Human nature being what it is, it feels good — it feels warm — to have the leader of a ministry talking to me on my computer screen — out loud, animated — when I visit his or her website. There's no escaping the feeling.

It has always been necessary, even before the Internet, for ministries to invest in relationships. "Prospecting" — employing strategies for finding new donors — has always been expensive on the front end. But without prospecting, a ministry is doomed. Eventually its donors will grow old and die, or move on to other interests. **Donors must be replaced.** Establishing relationships is the heart of prospecting. You can think of it as "loss" if you want to, but you must invest in relationship to make it happen — and trust God to provide.

Even massive media conglomerates have discovered this. Time Warner famously failed with its Pathfinder website, founded in October 1994. Among other problems, according to *Business 2.0*'s July 1999 issue, they simply "made the mistake of counting money spent on Pathfinder as losses rather than as what they were — investments in a new medium."

Paul wrote to the Christians at Philippi, "And my

God will meet all your needs according to his glorious riches in Christ Jesus" (**Philippians 4:19**). But what was the context of his remarks? He had just lauded them for their generous and faithful investment in his ministry. The message to us is clear: As we invest in ministry to people in need, God will meet our needs!

Scriptural Secret #13:

I need to learn to think about the other person's needs, not just my own.

"I am fascinated by my ministry."

This is true of most ministry leaders.

But there's a vital difference between being *fascinated* and being *fascinating*.

Most people in the world aren't fascinated by my ministry, even though I would love to believe they are.

The fact is, I'm a seller. That may sound crass, but my role as a ministry leader — most certainly as a ministry marketer — is a selling role: the role of the persuader. The donor, on the other hand, is the buyer. Crass, again, yes; but true. The donor is "buying in" to some proposition which I, as the marketer, am proposing.

All of which means, as a ministry leader or marketer **I can't be satisfied to design my website around things I think are fascinating. The buyer won't automatically be fascinated by what I, as the seller, find fascinating. I need to learn to think like the buyer, and render my ministry in some form that will be fascinating to him or her — not me.**

The apostle Paul in **Ephesians 4:29** advises that we should say "only what is helpful for building others up according to their needs, that it may benefit those who listen." The hearer, not the speaker, is the one intended to receive the benefit.

Hebrews 10:24 recommends that we "consider how we may spur one another on toward love and good deeds." It's significant that it does *not* recommend that we consider how to spur *ourselves* on toward love and good deeds. I already know what turns me on! There's no challenge to that, and little or no opportunity for spiritual growth. God's goal is to grow me spiritually — so He makes the *other* person a puzzle for me to figure out.

So often, however, our ministries attempt to "sell" ourselves to donors and prospective donors by simply telling them what *we* find important, interesting, or valuable. The "buyer" doesn't buy, however, unless something we present somehow meets a need that the *buyer* feels.

One classic example is the event promoter who puts a spot on the radio proclaiming "Plenty of good seats available!" I have taken to calling this syndrome POGSA because it's so common. The promoter is thinking like a seller — while the buyer, the listener, hears the POGSA message and says to himself, "This event is a dog; nobody's coming." It may be entirely true that plenty of good seats remain available. It may be a wondrous and valuable event to attend. But the seller has unintentionally communicated a selling concept instead of a buying concept.

To crack the code of the buyer's mindset is hard work. It isn't accomplished in one big brainstorming meeting. It's a continuous process; it's an ongoing effort. To think like the donor — resisting the tendency to think like the seller — must become a major commitment of a ministry leader and team. The issue must be re-visited every time communication with donors and prospects is addressed. The most successful ministries are those which make a sort of *lifestyle* out of "thinking like the buyer."

How much effort does your ministry expend in cracking the code of the buyer's perceived needs? The Web is perfect for this! Have you surveyed? Have you brainstormed the question? Is it possible that you have actually never considered the issue — or that you disdain the notion of catering to a prospect's needs? You wouldn't be alone. Many ministries only acquire as many donors as can be acquired by "luck" — the coincidental connection of the ministry's work with the interests of certain individuals who happen to cross its path. But how many more donors might be found, and might be inspired to get enthusiastically involved in supporting the work financially, if the ministry were presented in a way that they cared about?

When our agency creates a direct mail package or email appeal for a ministry, **we relentlessly push to find a lead paragraph for the letter which *involves* the reader. We look for an opening line that is actually about the *reader*, not just the ministry — featuring words like "you" and "yours."** Such an approach frequently fails to satisfy the ministry leader; there's a yearning to "get to the point." But the "point" for the ministry leader isn't the same as the "point" for the reader. The reader, even a relatively loyal donor, instinctively asks the question, "Why should I be bothered with this?" At that moment, the rest of that person's life is competing with the ministry for his or her attention. If your ministry's connection is being made via a website, the entire thrilling world of the Internet is beckoning. Competition for the individual's attention is *vicious*.

So you've got to talk to her *about her*. It's her favorite subject. And even if she eventually gives to your ministry with the purest of motives, she will still be doing so with a sense of *making a difference*. Ultimately, even the most selfless contribution has a selfish "I can make an impact" underpinning. This isn't sin — nor is it cynicism; it's just the way people are wired. In people who have given their lives to Christ, the Spirit of God cultivates this urge in a wholesome way. So can your ministry.

On a website, where demand for direct, straight-forward communication is much higher than in the mail, you'll do well to use phrases like these:

Get xxxxx free...

Receive xxxxx now...

Improve your xxxxx — Get xxxxx today...

Finally, you can xxxxx — Request your xxxxx here...

In other words, the more your website is about the visitor, the more effective it will be. "Taste the joy of feeding someone who's hungry" has more power than "Feed someone who's hungry." To those of us who have a heart for feeding the hungry, "Taste the joy" seems superfluous (especially to those of us "sellers" working in a ministry devoted to feeding the hungry). But to thousands of potential donors ("buyers"), who have their own lives to live — kids to get through school, cranky bosses to satisfy, marriages to navigate, medical and financial and emotional issues to deal with — a decree to "Feed someone who's hungry" doesn't have all that much automatic appeal.

This issue has never been more important than in the Age of the Net, because it is actually easier for an individual to bail out of a website than to bail out of a direct mail appeal letter package. **It takes more effort to throw away the carrier envelope, the letter, the reply device, and the reply envelope than it does to click on a single button and evaporate your website.** But if your website isn't connecting with the needs of the visitor, what reason does he or she have for staying? None. **Hebrews 10:24** turns out to be true, and practical, and *urgently necessary.*

Scriptural Secret #14:

God values long-term relationship. This is the essence of biblical community.

There's very little in the Bible promoting hit-and-run relationships. **Hebrews 13:1** says, in the New International Version, "Keep on loving each other as brothers." In the old days it was translated, "Let brotherly love continue." *Keep on — continue — meno*, if you want the original Greek. It's an *ongoing* concept.

My ministry's website needs to encourage long-term relationship. Perhaps we can think about it in terms of a fishing analogy — since Jesus, in **Matthew 4**, found Peter and Andrew "casting a net," and we now face the challenge of casting an *Internet*:

1. **Location.** I must get people to visit my site in the first place — so I must fish where the fish are. I have to advertise and register with search engines and do all the other things that Scriptural Secret #8 encouraged me to do.

2. **Lures.** Getting to the fish where they are is fine, but I also have to interest people in my ministry once they arrive at my site — so I offer something (inexpensive but) free that has high perceived value. I change lures often. Furthermore, since there's a sense that the Internet is vast, and a visitor typically wants to see way more of it than just my website, I arrange my site to "set the hook" in the visitor as quickly as possible.

3. **Hook.** The location is right? The lures are good? What a tragedy if people visit once and never come back. I need barbed hooks — the kind that keep the

fish on the hook — and the right bait, appealing bait, which will get people to *return* to my website.

How to draw visitors back? High energy helps — a website with fast-loading, vivid graphics and strong, punchy words. "Entertainment" — a taboo concept in many Christian circles — is the key. The visitor must find the website *interesting* compared to the average, low-energy, everyday website. Giving the visitor lots of attention also helps — plenty of opportunities to provide input and make a mark of some kind.

But perhaps the most important hook is the explicit promise of **something new to come**. If you offer a free booklet called *Faith-Builders for Your Family*, run a line underneath the request link that says, "Coming in October: *Solving Your Family Budget Questions!*"

The promise of something new to come can be implied as well, of course. At www.berkeybrendelsheline.com, we offer an instant free downloadable chapter of our book. The implication is that you can return to the site later and get a different chapter, although we don't say that outright.

Your website should certainly be offering the latest news about your ministry, and if you make it clear that the information you're presenting is indeed the latest news (a headline that says LATEST NEWS is a good indicator), anyone interested in your ministry's progress will have a reason to return. Keep in mind, though, that the latest news about your ministry only interests people already convinced that your ministry is worth their attention. The latest news about your ministry can't be your only hook because it won't work all by itself.

Include a survey of some kind that the visitor can fill out, and rotate the focus of the survey from month to month. Name the survey by the month in which it appears, and that will signal the visitor that your site will be different next month.

You should also continuously update the true-life stories of people touched by your ministry (see Scriptural Secret #9).

Some visitors will check back in at your site within a month even without hooks, but if they don't find fresh content, they're extremely unlikely to return.

All of which translates into time, money, energy, and expertise on the part of the ministry leadership and staff. The website must be tended to, or it will grow stale and repel donors. The "hooks" must be thought up, thought through, integrated with the rest of the ministry operation, designed into the site, posted, and followed up on. It's work. It's investment. But it's investment in long-term relationship with prospective donors — one of the most valuable investments you can make.

One of the Web-related questions that ministry teams often wrestle with is the question of target audience: For whom is the ministry's website intended? Should it target prospects, and try to steer them toward becoming donors? Should it target current donors, who will be likelier to give and cover the costs of the site — and simply let prospects "observe" the ministry and decide to join in if they want to?

The answer is not "either or," but "both and."

Certainly your website can be a leading tool for prospecting. People who come looking for your site are the most cost-effective prospects in the world, because they are people likely to be interested already in your issue.

But your website can also become the *primary gathering place for your ministry family*.

In years to come, as more and more donors spend more and more time online, they will "gather" at the various websites that reflect their lifestyle choices. They will "gather" (although not all at the same time) around football websites, for example, to learn about upcoming games, interact about past games, and even *watch* games. They will "gather" at church websites and needlepoint websites and how-to-help-your-kid-with-homework websites. The more closely identified with your ministry a donor is, the likelier he or she will "gather" at your website — if you provide a "home," a place of nurture and value, to gather at.

Your website can be both a "front door" for prospects and a "family room" for committed donors. Make the first page of your site almost totally first-time-visitor-oriented — featuring a free offer, for example — with an easy way for repeat visitors to bypass the offer and go to the "guts" of the site. (A button which simply reads "Jump right into the site" will do nicely.)

On the first "interior" page of your website, you can give visitors the opportunity to click on a simple button and **designate *that* page as their "home page"** — the page that automatically appears on their computer screen each time they open their browser. This decision lets your ministry site become the *first* place an individual visits each time he or she opens the browser program to go online.

You can also **invite the visitor to "bookmark" your site** — which means your site's address will be added to the list of favorites stored in the individual's browser.

The goal is not just to get more and more "hits" or visits by prospects and donors, but to *build an "online community."* You want to create a place where people *want* to spend time together, and bring others. (Add an "Email this to a friend" button to key features to encourage visitors to get the word out to others.) Post a "discussion board" on one page of your site — a place where people can comment and respond to others' comments. Arrange live chat times on specific topics.

("Chat" enables multiple visitors to type comments to each other "live" online.) Use the website to promote live events that the visitor can attend or become involved in (they can RSVP instantly via the website).

(If for any reason you want to make certain portions of your website available only to donors, it's possible to set up a membership arrangement, with the visitor typing in a password to gain access to the "insider information" sections of the site. But this will normally be unnecessary — and may annoy first-time visitors.)

Throughout the experience of your website, the visitor should have the impression of **high value**: receiving benefits, the potential to get products or services, news about the ministry, stories about people's lives being changed, and the opportunity to have a personal part in it all. Even when you are not offering a visitor an actual product in exchange for a contribution, you can offer the **"satisfaction of knowing you're making a difference"** — so fundamental and frequent a concept in ministry marketing that our agency staffers have come to refer to it as SOKYMAD.

This is not to suggest that you shouldn't ask for money. Give the visitor an opportunity to donate immediately, and don't apologize for it. The chance to give a donation toward the work should be a positive emotional moment — an opportunity presented in the midst of a lively, exciting environment. The basic phenomenon at work here is the idea of "value exchange": The ministry does great work and offers valuable products to the visitor (including the SOKYMAD), and the visitor provides the contributions that make it all possible.

This feeling — of *giving* as *opportunity* rather than, say, drudgery or obligation — can lead you to bold offers of even greater commitment on the part of the visitor. For example, your website can provide an **Automatic**

Funds Transfer (AFT) option, in which the visitor authorizes a certain gift amount to be withdrawn from his or her bank account automatically on a monthly schedule. (The arrangement is always instantly cancelable by the individual, so the risk is nil.) This allows you to establish a membership program which increases the commitment of your donors.

It may also be appropriate for you to sell merchandise outright, or offer merchandise for a "suggested contribution," via your website. This may be the only venue where it would feel right to offer, say, coffee mugs bearing the logo of the ministry or a photograph of the ministry leader — or even "generic" ministry products like Bibles and devotionals. Perhaps your website could include a "ministry bazaar" where you offer anything of value to your ministry family *as a service to them*. You could even allow individuals to post Help Wanted ads and vocational résumés on a special page of the site. **The more reasons you offer for visitors to return, the greater the sense of community you build — and the likelier you are to establish a relationship with a visitor which will involve financial support for your ministry.**

(Should your site target Christians or spiritual seekers? This is a question inextricably intertwined with your unique mission. Many skeptics visit the Internet sites of Christian ministries; how you account for their presence as visitors to your site must be determined in large measure by your ministry's unique vision and purpose. You may wish to offer one or more links to seeker-friendly sites like www.hopenet.net.)

If we stop designing our ministry websites around the question "How can we get donations?" and instead focus on "How can we serve the visitor?", we'll find ourselves developing longer-term relationships. And as you get the "serving" focus — as you learn to think like the "buyer," caring more about his or her needs than our own — your website will bear a number of small but important practical earmarks:

1. **You'll talk to one person at a time — literally.** The text on your website should be written for a sole reader. Never use phrases like "Many of you may be wondering ..." or "Many of you probably think ..." It should always be "You may be wondering ..." or "You probably think ..."

2. **You'll do as much of the work as possible for your visitor.** Program your order form, for example, to require basic information like name and addresses to be typed only once — and automatically re-appear elsewhere if it's needed a second time.

3. **You'll program your website to send an instant automatic email** confirming each significant action the visitor has taken — placing an order, giving an online donation, asking a question, whatever. Make your auto-responses warm and human, not cold and clinical. Let your visitors feel that they did the best possible thing by taking the action they took!

4. **You'll *add* value wherever possible.** If the visitor requests a book, send along with it, unannounced, a notepad or pencil or fridge magnet (bearing your logo and message, of course). If the visitor downloads a chapter of your book, include a devotional as a bonus. Let the visitor's expectations always be exceeded.

5. **You'll communicate in simple, informal, direct language.** The apostle Paul was committed to "setting forth the truth plainly" (**2 Corinthians 4:2**). We should be, too.

6. **You'll make sure your website is of the "easy access" variety.** Keep sentences and paragraphs very short; use bullets where you can. Don't just convert your printed pieces to HTML and post them — it's harder to read a screen than a printed page, so be kind to your visitor and simplify, simplify, simplify.

7. **You'll offer lots of photographs, but "optimized" so that they load quickly on the visitor's screen.** Vast expanses of text-only pages are uninspiring. But photographs are data-intense and will take a long, annoying time to appear on the visitor's screen unless they're optimized for the Web. Optimizing is a simple process which your webmaster should be able to accomplish as your photos are being posted to your website.

8. **You'll make each page of your site clean and easy to follow, not cluttered or complicated.** Don't make your visitor squint and search for information. Communicate that you care about the visitor's comfort by making it a simple pleasure to arrive at your site, scan the available choices, and gather information. And ...

9. **You'll overflow with gratitude.** Imagine how the visitor feels getting a thank-you note 20 seconds after he or she requests a product or donates to the ministry online. But why not build in a program that goes *back* to that person with a follow-up thank-you email a week later? The technology is there — it requires no additional manpower to send an automatic email — it requires only the creative imagination and will of the ministry team to set up the program in the first place.

In fact, it would be a waste of perfectly good technology to have a website that invites the visitor to share his or her email address — and then *not* send occasional emails to that person. It's illegal in some states to send requests for contributions via email without the prior permission of the recipient — the law is likely to change fast on this over the next couple years — but even without direct solicitations, emailing your previous website visitors can become one of the most valuable efforts you make as a ministry. (See Scriptural Secret #10.)

This is how two good friends would interact with each other. One would visit, the other would follow up with a letter or call. They would stay in touch. And a good friend is what you hope to become to that visitor. So organize your website to function in as friendly a way as possible.

Who Goes There?

Scriptural Secret #15:

For maximum effectiveness, count the cost; gauge your impact.

In a culture where buying on the installment plan is commonplace and debt is practically a status symbol, the ancient virtue of "counting the cost" (**Luke 14:28**) is a lost art.

Of course, responsible ministries gauge the effectiveness of their marketing strategies; but the process of gathering data, analyzing, and adjusting accordingly can be lengthy, cumbersome, and inefficient. In direct mail, for example, it takes weeks to produce and mail a package, get the responses, and analyze the cost-effectiveness of the effort. A telemarketing campaign can be adjusted more quickly, as the callers record donors' responses to the script being used. But the Internet allows you to track visitors' responsiveness to your website literally minute-by-minute — and adjust your presentation almost that quickly as well. You can change an appeal on your website every day if you want to, as the computer calculates the relative impact of each approach. Computers, after all, are essentially calculating machines — calculating is what they do best.

The Internet has spawned tracking mechanisms which make information ready, even instantly, available. A standard statistical measurement apparatus, simply and invisibly programmed into your website, can tell you at a glance not only

1. **how many visitors your site has had over various periods of time, but also**

   2. **how long they stayed,**
   3. **which pages of your site they visited and**
   4. **in what sequence —**
   5. **even what *other* website they visited just *prior* to visiting yours!**

This kind of information tells you which search engines, for example, are sending the most visitors your way. It also tells you literally how your website is working — what interests your visitors most, what's catching their eye as they arrive, how they travel through your site, and so forth.

But having the information available doesn't help if someone in your ministry isn't monitoring the results closely — and often. Are people skipping past the free screensaver download and moving directly to your construction project photo gallery? Is the free download button too small or out of the way? Is a screensaver unattractive? You can move or change the download button for a few days — and change the screensaver offer for a few days — and you may soon have a good idea of what the problem was.

If we value our relationships with our donors, we need to track their responses as a means of guiding us into *better service to them*. The Internet makes this goal totally accessible.

Data gathered via your website must be integrated with your donor giving records; but be sure to flag each donor account with an indicator of the "source motivation" — how the donor first arrived on the file. Your website will generate new donors, but they will be somewhat different in character from donors acquired by direct mail, telemarketing, television, radio, print advertising, or live events. Television ministries, for example, find that donors who join the cause after watching a TV special have different response patterns than donors who join the cause after receiving a direct mail appeal letter. Donors responding initially to one type of project or issue may reveal very different response rates to other projects or issues.

You may find that it's most cost-effective to communicate with various segments of your donor file in different ways, based on their source motivation. Don't expect to dump Internet-acquired names onto your existing mailing list and communicate to everybody in exactly the same way or on exactly the same themes. You'll be missing out on an opportunity to cultivate a deeper level of commitment on the part of your Internet family. What if some basic testing reveals that your Internet names respond far more generously to emailed appeals than to snail-mailed appeals? Counting the cost, gauging your impact, and adjusting accordingly will result in more efficient marketing of your ministry.

IV.
FIVE SECRETS OF IDENTITY

⎯⎯⎯ SpeedLink:

This section is for YOU if ...

- You're wondering which element of your website is **most important**
- Your ministry team differs on the question of "how **fancy**" or "how plain" to make your website
- The person in charge of your website **doesn't attend** most of your ministry marketing meetings
- You're unsure how direct to be in asking the donor to **give** via your website
- The whole Internet thing is **stressing** you out

Welcome to the Berkey Box

Scriptural Secret #16:

God gave you the vision for your ministry. Keep that picture clearly in focus. But as you communicate that picture to people, you must communicate in terms they can understand.

Jesus made the religious leaders nervous when He demonstrated His willingness to boil the entire Old Testament down to two commandments, in **Matthew 22:36-40**. They had spent their lives convincing people to obey a more and more complicated tangle of rules and regulations. Jesus reduced the entire machine of organized religion to less than five seconds' worth of truth: Love God, and love each other.

Ministry leaders today sometimes feel a bit like the

Pharisees did — when anyone suggests that they narrow the message of their ministry to a single thought, three sentences maximum. We don't like to think that our wonderful, thrilling, complex ministry — the work to which we are devoting our lives — can be reduced to a simple little nugget. For years our agency has recommended this painful process to ministries — the concept formed the heart of our book *Seven Deadly Diseases of Ministry Marketing* — and we have witnessed a serious amount of bloodshed among ministry team members as a result. (Leaders of Christian organizations have told us that this is one key reason why ministries should use outside marketing help.) Set out to pare down the message of your ministry to a single, simple thought, and you begin to discover just how unfocused your ministry team has been all along!

The "message" of your ministry is not your "mission statement" or "vision statement." A mission statement could be defined as *what you do*; your vision statement might be regarded as *where you're going*. But your *message* is the one idea that you are committed to expressing to donors and prospective donors. It's not just *what you do* or *where you're going*, because the donor doesn't care, deep down, what you do or where you go. The donor is consumed with his or her own life's problems.

So your ministry's message must be every bit as much about him or her as it is about you — in order to cut through the chaos of the donor's life and get him or her to pay some real attention to your ministry.

The message must be a single, simple thought that matters to the donor.

And because people in general are not nearly as tuned in to the importance of your ministry as *you* are, the message must be repeated endlessly — way past the limit of the ministry team's affection for it —

if there's any hope of it finally getting through to the donor.

Internet users are notoriously impatient. You've got about six seconds to engage the visitor and get your message across. That's even *less* than the amount of time you typically have to convince a person to open and read something you've mailed to his or her home. So your message must come through loud and clear — and quickly.

One crucial question is, How long does your site take to "load" — or appear on the visitor's computer screen? People tend to access ministry sites more often from home than from work, and people's home computers tend to be weaker and slower than business computers. "Do the pages on your site download in ten seconds with a 28.8 bps modem?" asks Fred Goss in his *What's Working* newsletter (May 1999). If not, they're not loading quickly enough. Use fewer photographs, optimize graphics if you haven't already, or shrink the graphics to load faster. Text loads ahead of graphics, and much more quickly — but if the text on any page of your site takes longer than ten seconds to load, you've got way, way too much text on that page! Cut it down, or break it into multiple pages if you have to keep it all.

While veterans of direct response marketing have labored for years to create intriguing "teasers" on the outer envelopes of direct mail packages, **the Internet is not a medium where teasers work.** Internet users are not tuned for "intrigue." This is a very direct, straightforward medium. Get your message right up front, and don't be cute about it. With a million other interesting websites to get to, your visitor is impatient. Without a clear, brief simple message to latch onto, that visitor is off in a few moments to www.cnn.com or www.goodhousekeeping.com or the auction site www.eBay.com.

But none of this advice is really practical if you haven't determined as a ministry team what your message is .

If your ministry provides life-saving widgets to desperately ill Hoosiers, that's your *mission* but not your *message*. If your goal is a widget for every sick person in Indiana, and an end to Hoosier illness, that's your *vision* but not your message. If you distribute the widgets through a network of committed volunteers using low-cost, low-maintenance bicycles, and those volunteers work in teams that gather quarterly for training conferences where the ministry supplies their lodging, meals, and training materials free of charge thanks to the donations of caring friends, that's your *strategy* but not your message.

Your message needs to be something simple that matters to the donor — like "You can give a widget — and ease a Hoosier's suffering." Or "Your love provides a widget — and saves a Hoosier's life." Or "Your love — our widgets — new hope for hurting Hoosiers."

Practically speaking, your message must fit inside what we call the "Berkey Box" — literally a rectangle 6 inches tall and 9 inches wide — in a font no smaller than

18-point Times (which is what this is).

Some have come to call this the "Benefit Box" — which is appropriate, since your message essentially communicates the key benefit to the prospective donor, the unique selling proposition of your ministry. (The more distinct your message is from that of other ministries, the likelier you will be to pick up supporters!)

The Berkey Box, in any case, is identical to the amount of space that a typical Internet user has available on his or her computer screen. The rest of the space is taken up with the browser "window," "banner" ads, "toolbars," and other stuff that you can't control.

(Remember, the visitor is coming to your website by way of a browser application like Netscape Navigator or Internet Explorer, and the browser window takes up a certain amount of space on the computer screen. The visitor also controls how big the type is on the screen, and if they turn the size up, you get *less* of your message into a given amount of space.)

Establish your message on the front page of your site, then repeat it in some fashion on every subsequent page. This might mean repeating a key phrase of it, or a meaningful logo representing it. You might put it in the same position on every page, so it's easily identifiable.

This strategy dovetails with our recommendation that your website open with a "splash page." This is not a typical "home page" full of basic information, but a relatively simple initial page featuring only the name and logo of your ministry and two options for the visitor: (1) request something free, or (2) jump into the site.

The basics of creating a message for your ministry are so important that our agency has published a poster on the subject, for ministries to display in their offices. You can download it for yourself, right now, via our website (www.berkeybrendelsheline.com/message), or print it out, duplicate it, or otherwise transfer it from the following:

BERKEY BRENDEL SHELINE

The Message

is more important than the mechanics of communicating it.

The Message

must compete with thousands of other matters intruding on the donor's attention.

The Message

therefore must be repeated constantly, in terms that the donors understand, and in ways that make it count *for them*.

Ministry Development Specialists
www.berkeybrendelsheline.com

Scriptural Secret #17:

Excellence is a virtue. Try to do ministry "cheap," and you'll forfeit ministry opportunities.

How fancy? How plain? Should my ministry's website look like a Broadway production? Or a humble storefront outpost?

The slaves of Colosse — a declining Turkish city in the days of Paul the apostle — could have been excused for doing shoddy work for their masters, who were by and large corrupt pagans or carnal Christians. Paul nevertheless admonished them to strive for excellence. "Whatever you do, work at it with all your heart," he said in **Colossians 3:23**, "as working for the Lord, not for men."

A website is, by its nature, a graphic presentation. Graphics are art, and art is a matter of taste. No one can dictate your taste — but if you're trying to communicate with great numbers of people (as you are, via your website), it's wise to take stock of the multitudes' taste. This translates to a policy of letting graphics be determined by people who know and understand such things. **One of the deadliest formulas in ministry marketing is for art or graphic design to be steered by a theologian, a writer, or an administrator — someone who forgets the target audience, or lets his own taste dictate.**

Christian ministries and their websites should reflect a commitment to true excellence. Don't let your volunteer brother-in-law design your site unless he's a professional website designer of some standing. Invest in the design of your website.

Our agency has invested in the support of proven Web design professionals, headed by the Internet veteran Carol Tuominen, www.networks-consulting.com. If you're uneasy about managing the design of your website, we'll help you. It's natural, of course, to want *not to need* help. It's human nature to desire self-sufficiency. This is why many ministry teams squander precious time, energy, and resources trying to become experts at various specialties — staffing up huge art departments, or data management departments, or whatever — instead of forming partnerships with reliable specialists in these fields. Of course some ministries succeed in becoming expert in certain off-the-beaten-path specialties. But Internet graphic design isn't often one of them. As a matter of stewardship, it's usually wiser to hire the design of your website from someone who devotes his or her life to this kind of work.

When it comes to website design, it's important to understand the difference between art and science. Many ministries make the mistake of letting "scientists" — computer-oriented individuals who understand the posting process — do the *art*, the *design*, of their website. This hardly ever works. It's rare to find a "computer nerd" who's also artistic. But hiring someone to post a website for you (and there are 14-year-olds who can do this) is usually much less expensive than hiring someone to *design* a website and do it *well*.

Amateurish sites are easy to spot. They often feature busy, almost "madcap" arrangements of text and images. The typical visitor will not respond positively to amateurish graphic design — because so much of the Internet already features polished, professional graphic design.

This doesn't mean your ministry has to invest heavily in expensive graphic design. It simply means the look of each page must be simple and clean — which is actually quite tricky for someone who's not really an artist.

At the very least, your entire site should conform to a **single graphic motif**. Make all the backgrounds the same simple color or pattern — nothing too distracting, and nothing that makes the text difficult to read. Basic principles of good text and image presentation must be adhered to: If possible, settle on a **single font** if you can. If you can, keep all your headlines, the **same size** throughout the site; likewise with subheads and body text. Build each page from the **same basic layout**: text beginning the same distance from the left edge, spacing between paragraphs standardized, etc.

And more important than any other guideline, make absolutely sure that whatever you put on the screen is *readable*. The average visitor to your website can't be guaranteed to have good eyesight, let alone a guaranteed inclination to be interested in what you have to say. So any *obstacle* to readability is an invitation to go *bye-bye*.

It does not take a dancing, singing, flashing website to grab and hold a visitor. But it is extremely difficult to re-capture a visitor who has already encountered tacky amateurism at your website. Commit yourself to excellence from the beginning.

Scriptural Secret #18:

Integrity demands consistency. All the components of a life (or a ministry) must be integrated with each other, all representing the same central value.

Jesus healed people and told them to keep quiet about it. He also healed people and placed no such restriction on them. He had different strategies for different times of His life, different objectives of His ministry. Yet Christ's identity, His character and mission, were unchanging. "Jesus Christ is the same yesterday and today and forever," **Hebrews 13:8** declares.

Paul was "all things to all people" (**1 Corinthians 9:22**). His tactics changed from situation to situation, based on the audience and the need. Yet his life and ministry were unified in Christ.

Christian ministries today tend to misunderstand and mishandle the balance between these two seemingly contradictory concepts. My style must fluctuate; my substance must not. Your ministry is a single entity, and must be perceived by the prospective donor as a single entity no matter what medium happens to be in use at the moment.

Some organizations commit themselves to such rigid unity of presentation that they fail to communicate effectively at all in certain media. A publisher of Christian books, for example, might get so stuck in the rather formal, intellectual lingo of the printed page that it winds up producing dry, ineffective television promotions.

More often, however, organizations fragment along

tactical lines. The TV group sits in one room, the direct mail group in another, the live events group in another — and each gradually develops its own message. In extreme cases, the ministry ends up promoting one idea to one audience and a completely distinct idea to another audience. The drive to be all things to all people — communicating to TV viewers via TV, for example, and readers via print — swamps the need for integration. The ministry team is fragmented internally, and the impact of the ministry's message is diminished among donors.

Because the Internet is relatively new, even reasonably well integrated ministries often suffer from "isolated Internet operation" syndrome. The various functions of the ministry organization may be talking to each other — Operations is on the same page as Public Relations, Marketing is in synch with Accounting, and so forth — but the Internet functions are off in a low-priority corner somewhere.

It's crucial that the ministry's Internet presentation be integrated with the rest of the ministry. If anything, staff responsible for the website need to know *first* about any new developments in the ministry, because updates to the website need to be timely. (There's nothing like stale news on your website to make your ministry look disorganized, careless, and amateurish.)

Meanwhile, **the presentation of the ministry in various other media — TV, radio, print, mail, the phones, events — should be coordinated with the presentation of the ministry on the Internet**. If I'm a visitor to your website, I should get a similar "read" on your ministry — the language, the graphics, but more importantly the message and the news — as I get when I tune in to your program, or read your magazine, or receive an appeal letter from you. A fresh, dynamic feel in a printed piece is contradicted — and the overall effect undermined — if I look you up on the Web and find you to be boring and outdated.

> Next time you find yourself sitting in a meeting with the staff members responsible for your ministry's various communication streams, look around and ask, "Who's missing?" If the person in charge of your website is absent, it's time to add one name to your guest list.

Synergy is a powerful marketing force. If your website can focus on the same project, theme, campaign, or offer as your TV, radio, print, phone, and live-event efforts, you'll multiply the power of each communication stream. Ideally, over the course of, say, six weeks, I should encounter promotion of your "Shoes for the Shoeless" campaign in a direct mail letter package or two, the latest issue of your magazine or newsletter, a telephone solicitation, your TV or radio program, space ads in newspapers or magazines, cards in card decks, your ministry leader's speaking engagements, the "shoe fair" you sponsor on the parking lot of your ministry facility — and, most certainly, on the splash page of your website!

If you're offering a product in exchange for a donation, and you don't want current donors to swamp you with requests when they see your promotions to the general public, pitch the product to your house file first. But in most ministries, the number of likely responders is low enough that a frenzy of donations would constitute a *good* problem to endure.

Help! I Need Somebody!

Scriptural Secret #19:

Telling the truth, even to the point of revealing your needs, is a virtue.

Would you rather go to a picnic — or paint the house?

No contest. We love the good times, and would rather not have to do the work.

But eventually the house has got to be painted. Ultimately, it gets so ratty-looking that people would be embarrassed to visit!

Your ministry's website cannot be the picnic only — the paint job must also happen. Sure, you should focus on making your website a fun, energetic, upbeat place where people want to gather, a place where your ministry family develops a sense of "community." But you also have to be honest with visitors about what you need.

According to my natural human tendency, I don't want you to know that I need anything at all. But at its core, that's pride. I want you to think of me as better — more self-sufficient, of higher quality — than I really am.

It's a deadly route. "For whoever exalts himself," Jesus says in **Matthew 23:12**, "will be humbled."

If you fail to reveal your need, you are very likely to suffer all the side-effects of *unmet needs*.

On the other hand, if you're willing to make your ministry transparent and vulnerable, you'll find that God provides. "Whoever humbles himself," Jesus goes on to say, "will be exalted."

Since God designed people to give to each other, He promotes His design by meeting needs through people's giving. Giving cultivates relationships, and relationships are the heart of the biblical concept of community . God's great goal for His people here on earth is that we will "be one" (**John 17:20,21**). That's a picture of community — relationships in action. A system of *giving* to meet one another's needs *fosters* those community-building relationships.

All of which tells us that we need to see the donor's support for the ministry as *not only* good for the *ministry*, but *also good for the donor*. Moreover, it is an exercise in spiritual maturity for the ministry to admit to its own need.

So — bottom line: **Ask for money.**

When a visitor cruises through your website, donating to the cause should be one of the significant opportunities made available.

But generic donations for generic causes won't inspire many visitors to your website. The more specifically you can describe your need, and the more specifically you can describe how a donation will be used, the likelier you are to receive a gift. "Give $24 to provide a mat, blanket, and pillow to a child in our new clinic in Bangkok" beats "Please donate to our ministry."

There's always the dilemma of asking for "designated funds." Ethics and the law require that money solicited on the basis of one project not be used for another project without the blessing of the donor. (This is why we so often see "disclaimer" language added to appeals for specific projects — like "and to continue all of our ministry's other outreaches.") But there's far more power in a targeted appeal; asking for designated funds almost always gets a bigger response than asking for general funds. Still, you have a bunch of stuff to *do* as a ministry (unglamorous stuff like paying the light bill and replacing worn-out office chairs for your staff) which can't be done with designated funds. This tension is difficult to resolve in expensive, unwieldy fundraising venues like direct mail or television.

But on the Internet — at least for the time being — you're unlikely to get a huge response. In fact, it will probably be years before you generate a significant percentage of your ministry's overall revenues via your website. This means that you can afford to isolate website income on specific projects.

So go ahead and **ask for designated money on your website**. Ask for $26,000 for recording the New Testament in a whole new language. Ask for $4 to give a Bible to someone. Tell visitors that $50 will provide the *Book of Hope* to 150 school children in their own languages. Note that $37 gives the New Testament on audio tape to "Bibleless" people in another land.

In conventional direct mail, it's always wise to isolate a single need in a single mailing. But on your website, you have more freedom. You can offer a menu of projects (one button for each, so the visitor can go to a separate page of the site for more information about any one of them). Your website also gives you the opportunity to ask for donations of goods — the kind of request which would distract if it were included in a direct mail package appealing for funds. (One more advantage to designated asks on your website: You can gauge donor interest in very specific areas in very short order.)

Crises can actually become blessings, too. To reveal a setback or unexpected problem on your website probably won't gratify your sense of self-esteem, but it can be refreshing to the one who learns the news. Say what's actually happening in your ministry — good and bad alike — and people may actually be surprised and pleased.

The Internet is an environment of greater candor, informality, and accountability than the world of direct mail, television, or radio. Cynical and skeptical Web surfers feel freer to ask questions about your ministry via the Internet — and they expect the results of fundraising drives to be reported. On a major drive requiring several weeks, you can actually show the daily total on your website — a boon to your credibility as a high-integrity organization.

If your ministry isn't a member of ECFA, the Evangelical Council for Financial Accountability (www.ecfa.org), join. For some 20 years, ECFA has evaluated the financial integrity of charitable organizations. This kind of accountability is even more important in the Internet Age, because the newness of the Internet phenomenon appears to be encouraging more and more unscrupulous and fraudulent pseudo-charities to prey on unsuspecting prospective donors. As a member in good standing of ECFA, you'll be able to post the ECFA logo on your website — a seal of approval which offers real security to prospective donors. (And make the ECFA seal a link to the ECFA website.)

One more credibility-builder: Promise privacy. Declare clearly as you ask for donations, "Your privacy is important to us. We will not share any information about you with any other organization." This commitment on your part, clearly stated as you ask for help, will deepen the visitor's sense of security, and increase your chances of receiving the gift.

Yes, your overall website can feel like a picnic — but when the house needs painting, ask for help. Telling the truth, even when it's not all good news, is a good thing.

Scriptural Secret #20:

Have fun. Be joyful. Be courageous. Be inventive and creative.

Some people think of God's Law as hard, mean, cold, narrow, difficult. Christians, then, are supposed to be dark, glum, solemn, cool, somber.

If we're stuck in that perception, we're missing the point.

God's design produces safety; so it should produce joy — delight — laughter — fun!

That is, if we're really living by God's design, and not some flawed human *version* of God's design.

When God's ideal had so long fallen out of favor with the nation of Israel that the Scriptures had to be *re-introduced* to the people, Governor Nehemiah and Reverend Ezra set out to have the whole thing read aloud to the entire population. The people, recognizing how they had blown it, were glum.

Wait — Nehemiah and Ezra said to them — this is not the intended result. "Do not mourn or weep," they said in **Nehemiah 8:9,10**. Joy is supposed to follow repentance. "Go and enjoy choice food and sweet drinks, and send some to those who have nothing prepared," they advised the people. "The joy of the Lord is your strength."

In other words, the thing that makes you strong — the thing that will set you apart, make people look at you and ask, "What *is* it about that person that makes me want what *they* have?" — is *joy*. It's the fruit of the Spirit! Not your supposed status as a slave under a cosmic Slavemaster. Not your dutiful obedience to a long list of do's and don'ts. But the sheer delight — the fun — the exhilaration of living in the *fullness* of God's original design for your life! "I have come that they may have life," Jesus declared in **John 10:10**, "and have it *to the full*."

That's the spirit that needs to pervade our lives and our ministry websites, not to mention our ministries themselves. If you are living in the "joy of the Lord," show it in your ministry. Show it in the way you express your ministry. Show it in your website.

The Internet is new and strange enough to many of us that we instinctively retreat into "What is everybody else doing?" mode. We want to be safe, to minimize our risk, to avoid looking foolish. So we do our best to create the same kind of website that everybody else is creating. But the Internet thrives on the fresh, the new, the different, the out-of-the-ordinary, the strange, the odd, the slightly-off-balance, the surprising. Be brave. Find your own niche.

For ministry leaders who have made careers out of being conventional, this may mean *turning a little loose* of the staff members responsible for the website. It may mean taking a deep breath and letting them try new twists and turns — giving it 30 days to see how the website's visitors respond.

The visitor to your ministry's website should want to return because it was such a stirring experience. But if visiting your ministry's website is relatively the same as visiting another ministry's website, your conservatism is radically shrinking your marketing potential.

"Dare to be different," Weintraut and Davis advised in the July 1999 issue of *Business 2.0*. They were addressing commercial entrepreneurs, but the principle applies to ministries as well: Too many fall into the "common trap" of merely putting a "digital storefront on an old-world business" and expecting to strike it rich.

The experts' advice: "Surprise others before they surprise you."

Your website, because it's so easy to change from day to day, is the perfect place to take some chances with how you express yourself — and see what happens!

V.
FIVE SECRETS OF THE HARVEST

═══ SpeedLink:

This section is for YOU if ...

- Your team members can't seem to **agree** on how to present your ministry
- You can't imagine someone ***not* loving** your ministry
- You wonder exactly **how to ask** a visitor to your website for a donation — and **how often**
- You're wondering what, if anything, to **"offer"** the visitor as they make their contribution
- You feel a certain gap between the "spiritual" work of your ministry and the **"fleshly"** fundraising work of your website

---

Get Out of Jail Free

Scriptural Secret #21:

Sowing seed is an essential step in the farming cycle. You can't just harvest.

Thanks to the Internet, 50 ministries have gotten out of prison.

For years, our agency has pushed Christian ministries to behave within the law of direct-response marketing which dictates that an appeal — in the mail, on the phone, or in a TV or radio spot — must be about *one thing only.* The reality is that an individual's attention to an appeal is typically so marginal that any dilution of the request or distraction from the main theme will almost inevitably diminish response. In other words, don't muck up an appeal letter about feeding hungry

children by inserting a brochure about your estate
planning department. And don't tell all about the
logistical details of your operation; keep the focus on the
compelling emotional issues and necessary facts.
Ministry staffers feel like we've put them in jail when we
insist that they must distinguish between direct response
mechanisms and information dissemination mechanisms.
They love their ministries and want to tell *all about them*
at every opportunity. But this is the real world: An
appeal letter or a telemarketing call is designed for
response, and can't serve efficiently as an educational
device.

On the other hand, not every communication from
your ministry can be a response mechanism. Information
about your ministry must be communicated to your
donors. Education about your work must occur. Donors
and prospects must come to understand that you are
not simply using them as a funding source, but that you
are actually entering into a relationship — a value
exchange — with them. If they come to feel that every
time they hear from you, it's just to be solicited for a
donation, they'll withdraw quickly. "A sluggard does not
plow in season," says **Proverbs 20:4**; "so at harvest
time he looks but finds nothing." You must provide
information, insight, inspiration — you must invest in
the individual before you can expect a return.

**A website offers the best of both the response
world and the info-world.** You can make a simple,
straightforward offer to your visitor on your splash page,
but fill the subsequent pages of your site with a great
volume of information. The visitor is free to browse,
gathering as much or as little information as is desired.
If the information you're sharing is fascinating — and
the site is easy to navigate — that visitor may be
convinced to become a donor before the visit is over!

Scriptural Secret #22:

Sometimes people are ripe, sometimes they aren't. Each encounter is another impression, a link in the chain of the relationship.

Not all the sinners respond to every altar call. Not all the viewers buy in response to the first commercial. Not all the girls — or guys — fall in love on the first date.

We're talking $\boxed{process}$ here.

A chain of impressions, linked together over time — perhaps the friendly witness of a neighbor, a Christian book, a radio program, an invitation to a special event at a church — finally lead a sinner to give his or her life to Christ.

A chain of impressions, linked together over time — maybe a TV spot, a radio spot, an ad in *Time* magazine, a sign in a store window, maybe a *dozen* more TV spots — finally lead the customer to buy.

A chain of impressions, linked together over time — "the way you hold your hat, the way you sip your tea," Ira Gershwin might say — finally lead to love, marriage, and baby carriage.

And a chain of impressions, linked together over time, finally leads an individual to become a donor to your ministry.

It's called (not surprisingly) the $\boxed{\text{"principle of}}$ $\boxed{\text{multiple impressions."}}$

Not everybody with an interest in the outcome can serve as the $\boxed{final}$ link in the chain, consistently "closing the sale" — not in evangelism, not in sales, not in romance. Different people, in different situations, at

different times, function as the [first] link — making the
very first impression on someone which eventually leads
them to a significant decision. But far more people, far
more frequently and in far more situations, function as
one of many [intermediate] links in the chain.

Paul the apostle experienced this, and referred to it
in **1 Corinthians 3:6**: "I planted the seed," he observed,
"Apollos watered it...." Paul was the first link in the
chain. Apollos provided a number of intermediate links.

Your website, with its mixture of information
offered and responses requested, stands an excellent
chance of serving as multiple links in the chain. It stands
a much *smaller* chance of actually serving as the *final* link,
providing the first-time giving opportunity that the
visitor finally seizes.

In large measure, this is true for the same reasons
that the principle of multiple impressions is true: The
average visitor to your website is:

1. **relatively busy** — eager to get on to other
   things in his or her life, probably including
   other websites
2. **relatively bored** — not as interested in your
   ministry as *you* are (see Scriptural Secret #13),
   and
3. **a relatively bad reader** (good readers gravitate
   to jobs as *creators* of reading content — they're
   writers, in essence — and don't naturally think
   in terms of anyone having lower reading skills)

These characteristics translate into "fuzzy message
transfer." You make your message 100% clear, and it only
makes, say, a 15% clear impact on the reader. So you
have to keep after it. You have to give that reader more
of the same impression. If the visitor returns a second
time, his or her impression of your message may be

clearer — but conventional wisdom says a commercial sale is made around the *seventh* impression (which is why you see the same commercial over and over during a single football game). In any case, the buyer — commercial or charitable — probably isn't "ripe" to "buy" on most visits to your website.

Since it's not possible to force the ripening of the visitor (we can only *encourage* it), the best alternative is to provide a delightful, entertaining, intriguing, valuable, multi-faceted, ever-changing environment for the visitor to wander through. Grow a relationship with them, give them information, involve them with your website and your ministry, so that over time they acquire enough clarity about your message that they can make a decision to support your cause with a donation. **The more choices you can give the visitor — without cluttering any individual page too much — the better your chances of holding that visitor until (or motivating that visitor to return at) the point of ripening.**

Your website's tracking program (see Scriptural Secret #15) will show you how many "hits," or visits, your site is getting — and the average time a visitor spends at the site. Your online contribution apparatus will show you how many dollars, and dollars per donation, you're receiving. But it's the *comparison* of these two figures that will tell you a lot about the | *fundraising efficiency* | of your site. In the same way that direct mail prospecting is a high-risk, low-initial-return venture — consider yourself very lucky if you get | 1% return | on a donor acquisition mailing to a rented list — your website will probably not produce a deluge of contributions.

If you're getting one donation out of every 100 hits, consider yourself a genius. You're getting them, and picking them, ripe!

Scriptural Secret #23:

To harvest, you have to put the blade to the crop. God doesn't do it for you by magic. You have to yank the fruit off the vine. You have to take invasive action.

If Satan cooks poison, he makes it with lots of sugar.

He'd love to get people so full of sweetness that they're unable to do the right thing when doing the right thing is bitter business.

A lot of ministry leaders find it distasteful to ask for money. They prefer to "love people" into giving.

But that ain't love — and it doesn't raise money.

Their ministries suffer because they're unwilling to invade the comfortable bubble of a person's world and challenge them to step out and accomplish more with their lives than what they're already accomplishing.

Ask for money. Make your request clear and simple. You have a valid ministry, and God's plan for funding it at least partially — and probably largely — involves the giving of His people.

In **Mark 4:26-29**, Jesus tells a parable which is often overlooked because it's so short and simple. The kingdom of God, He says, is like a man who "scatters seed on the ground." The seed grows around the clock, whether the sower is awake or asleep, whether he understands *how* it grows or not. "Night and day, whether he sleeps or gets up, the seed sprouts and grows, though he does not know how." Grain appears: "first the stalk, then the head, then the full kernel in the head." What does the farmer do? Sit and look at it? Paint a picture of it? Tell his friends about it? No. "As soon as the grain is ripe," Jesus says, "he puts the sickle to it, because the harvest has come."

And that is the entire parable. No plot twists, no elaborate explanations. We won't always know what is happening in someone's life on their way to a harvest-time decision. Romance is like this; evangelism is like this; sales are like this — and fundraising is like this. But "as soon as the grain is ripe," we've got to be ready to take action. When a visitor to your website turns out to be ripe, you've got to be ready to put the sickle in. You've got to ask for money.

A simple button — **"Donate here"** — may do the job. Make sure that this button is readily available throughout your site, however. But give your visitor an opportunity to learn more about a certain need, exploring a number of interior pages that describe in words and pictures what you're planning, and why it will cost money. Include a page of your site that explains where your funding comes from — a pie chart revealing sources, and another chart revealing expenditure categories. If you have nothing to hide with regard to your financial situation, then be bold in asking for support.

Always keep in mind that God designed people to love, to give, and they are going to be more satisfied in aligning with God's design as they seek the areas where God intends them to love, to give, to make contributions — financial and otherwise. The apostle Paul asked the Philippians for help, and then added, "Not that I am looking for a gift, but I am looking for what may be credited to your account" (**Philippians 4:17**).

This needs to become the heart of our requests for contributions.

Jesus was straightforward when it came to the

hardships that true disciples would face in this life. In the last ten verses of **Luke 14**, He talks about having to "hate" the things of this world, "give up everything," and so on. But He still urged people to go ahead, count the cost, and become His disciples — because He knew that there was a greater good to be experienced in that kind of life. We should also be courageous in asking visitors to invest some of their money in our ministries — because of the good it will do *them* as well as our ministries and those we serve.

Yes, it's work to ask for money. It takes real sensitivity and effort to do it well, to overcome the emotional obstacles, to deal with (often wrong-headed) misunderstandings and complaints, and to keep a balance between servanthood (the "We're here to bless you" emphasis) and leadership (the "You need to give" emphasis). But this work is necessary, and it is healthy to pursue.

In our evangelistic efforts, in our local church ministries, in our Christian charities, in the mail and on the phone, by TV and radio and in print — and yes, on our websites — we must do not just the planting work, not just the fertilizing work, but also the sometimes-uncomfortable *harvesting* work.

Scriptural Secret #24:

Reaping is simpler than nurturing the crop — but the harvest only happens if the crop has indeed been properly nurtured. Yes, you have to ask, but you also have to communicate intelligently and effectively.

It is unwise to run a vacuum sweeper in a corn field. That machine is unlikely to harvest your corn effectively.

How many movies have featured the otherwise delightful and attractive male coming to the point of proposing to the woman of his dreams, only to stumble awkwardly through a clumsy, ridiculous speech?

At the end of the ripening process, when it's finally time for reaping, the harvest must be conducted appropriately. Rex Humbard began his ministry as the "reaper" for his evangelist-father; the old man would preach, then sit down — and Rex would take over. He simply had a gift for "closing the sale." When he moved his simple but powerful approach to global television, millions came to faith in Christ as a result.

The principles related to sowing and reaping are part of God's design for our material, agricultural world, but we have observed that they also apply in a number of ways to other realms of life — not only evangelism, but also to fundraising for ministries.

Fortunately, a ministry website does not necessarily require an elaborate, mysterious apparatus for requesting donations. The straightforward "Donate" button (or "Donate now," or "Make your personal contribution," or whatever works for your ministry) may

suffice. Giving the visitor an opportunity to give to a
variety of individual projects is better yet. It can't hurt to
add an option for the visitor to sign on as a monthly
partner.

The actual harvesting of the gift, then, is — in and
of itself — pretty simple. Make sure the website provides
a secure means of transferring the donor's credit card
information. Be sure to communicate clearly that you
won't release their name, email address, or any other
information to any other organization. Give a toll-free
phone number for the Internet-wary. And offer an easy-
to-print-out form that someone could fax if they prefer,
or mail with a check if they wish. Other than that, the
harvest itself is really quite uncomplicated.

But the harvest only occurs *if you have prepared the
way effectively*. The visitor arrives essentially "ignorant" of
your ministry, at least probably. Your website gives the
visitor an opportunity to become educated; and the
effectiveness of your presentation (a clear message
communicated on clean, easily navigable pages) inspires
the visitor to take you up on that education opportunity.

Paul saw the principle in action in the spiritual
realm. He observed how his own audience advanced
over time in matters of spiritual education. "I could not
address you as spiritual but as worldly — mere infants
in Christ," he said in **1 Corinthians 3:1,2**. "I gave you
milk, not solid food, for you were not yet ready for it.
Indeed, you are still not ready."

The writer of Hebrews lived with the same reality,
trying to explain Christ's role as high priest: "We have
much to say about this, but it is hard to explain because
you are slow to learn. In fact, though by this time you
ought to be teachers, you need someone to teach you
the elementary truths of God's word all over again. You
need milk, not solid food!" (**Hebrews 5:11,12**).

The underlying frustration is clear: Both passages

seem to say, "Hurry up and learn!"

Yet in both passages, the teacher dutifully offered milk where milk was needed. In spite of the longing to see the student advance more quickly — for the student's own good — the teacher provided the education in a format *accessible* to — *effective* for — the student in question.

These passages clearly speak to discipleship, not fundraising. Yet the same spirit must guide our website designs. We must not assume the advanced commitment to our ministry, or understanding of our ministry, on the part of the visitor. We have to make as much information and inspiration available as we can, in a package that's accessible and appealing.

There's an art to designing a website that's easily navigable and attractive while still offering tons of information. Any page with too much text or graphic content will be slow loading and hard reading. So your website will need to be crafted around categories of information, with a reasonable amount of text and graphics on each page. Create a main menu which lets the visitor choose major categories of information, and as necessary provide additional sub-menus on interior pages. Well designed websites often have the most important links available on *all* the pages of a site, perhaps across the top or the left edge of the screen. (Rule of thumb: Make the information *available* but *not in the way.*)

A few practical suggestions:

1. **The typical user will not keep searching for desired information within a site after three clicks of the mouse.** This means the most crucial components of the site — links indicating *what's inside* — must be strategically positioned close to the "surface," the home page.

2. **Pages within the site must be designed with convenient links to subsequent pages within the site.** (For example, the site must *not* require the user to click his browser application's own "back" or "previous" key, something commonly seen in amateurish sites. Provide "go back," "go home," and other convenient directional buttons for your visitor — to signal that you have taken care to make the experience pleasant.

3. **Not knowing how soon a visitor might "ripen," capture the prospective donor early, by way of that free offer — or at least a product sale, if it's not possible to offer something free.** (Our agency website, www.berkeybrendelsheline.com, offers a book for sale, but in combination with one free chapter, which is immediately downloadable.)

4. **You can offer a compelling challenge to contribute on the spot — on the home page — by credit card via the Internet.** This is not likely to generate a large volume of gifts, but it does provide a convenience for previous visitors who return after a time with the intention of making a contribution; they don't have to go searching for a "Donate" button. (Your email list should be integrated with your donor database if possible, so your email communications can be planned and analyzed in light of your overall donor communication strategy.)

5. **Try to offer *both* a product which must be mailed by conventional mail *and* a product which can be emailed** (like an e-zine; see Scriptural Secret #10 and #11). This captures the visitor's street address (making subsequent direct mail contact possible) as well as the visitor's email address (making subsequent proactive email contact possible). The email address will become more and more valuable as time goes by, since you can let people know about

other opportunities very cheaply via email. Eventually your list of email addresses may rival the size of your conventional mailing list!

6. **Don't necessarily limit yourself to making just one offer.** A single strong offer can be featured on the front end of the visit, with additional offers available deeper into the site. (Maybe a free offer up front, with paid offers inside. Maybe offer a catalog.)

7. **"Get to know our staff" or "our ministry team" — the kind of feature which affirms your hard-working employees — needs to go deeper in the website**, where the information is available but not in the way. The average visitor, seeking "milk, not meat," won't want to go there. This is also true of the more detailed explanations of your ministry's operations and logistics.

We often find that the navigational design which *seems* ideal for a website soon turns out to be awkward or impractical in some unexpected way. A tracking program will show you how visitors are moving around in your site, how long they're spending on certain pages, which pages they're ignoring altogether, and which page is the *last* one they read (which may mean that this page is for some reason a curiosity-*killer*).

Fortunately, adjusting the navigation routes of a website is relatively easy — a far simpler and cheaper process than revising, say, a major brochure, reprinting it, and re-mailing it. Give yourself permission to adjust your website as often as necessary. By tinkering with your site until it's fluid — pleasant to experience, inviting to browse through — you're telling your visitors that you want to sow good things into their lives, not just reap good things out of them.

Scriptural Secret #25:
....
Going to people on behalf of God is important — but so is going to God on behalf of people!

I love the feeling of being in "God's work." I love helping ministries accomplish the stuff God has called them to accomplish. I love being a part of the process that enables ministries to communicate their God-given vision to people, helping people grasp the potential of that vision and become involved in making it actually happen.

But going to people on behalf of God isn't the only important thing. It's also important to go to God on behalf of people — and in our ministries, we often seem to forget or ignore this component. Yes, the apostle Paul in his work for the Lord said "Help me" to his Christian friends; but he also, in his work for people, said "Help them" to God.

Do you pray for your ministry family? Do you pray that God will draw your donors not only closer to the heart of your ministry, but closer to Him? Do you let them _know_ you're praying for them? (It certainly _would_ be dishonest to say you were praying if you weren't — but it would certainly be better to make some arrangement to pray for those who support your ministry financially.)

Some ministry leaders avoid talking with their donors about the prayers of the ministry staff because they don't want to look as if they're "selling prayer" — trading prayer for contributions. This may be valid; but what does it say about your ministry if your donors are likely to see your communication on this subject as a merchandising strategy? Perhaps your donors have become conditioned to seeing your organization as a marketing entity instead of a ministry entity. Your relationship with your donors may need a significant overhaul, so that they sense a deep and real caring about them on the part of your ministry.

For decades our agency has recommended to ministries that the staff pray regularly, specifically, and fervently for the ministry's donors. This is as much an exercise in spiritual growth for the staff as it is a benefit to the donors. **Certainly, prayer changes things: It changes both the one being prayed *for*, and the one doing the pray*ing*!**

Today, in the Age of the Internet, you can expand on this spiritually healthy process. Could you become comfortable offering your website visitors an opportunity to share their needs via email, so your staff can pray for them specifically? You may find enough visitors taking advantage of this opportunity that you have to distribute prayer requests among your various staff members — but even so, you can say with integrity on your website that members of your staff will pray for each need specifically. To someone in need, this could be an extremely meaningful and valuable kindness.

Could you become comfortable *responding* via email to website visitors' prayer requests? Imagine the impact of a visitor expressing a need via your website and receiving not only a generic automated reply (see Spiritual Secret #11 and #14), but later a *personal* emailed note from one of your staff members. "Just a brief note to let you know I prayed about your loved one's salvation" would not only serve as a source of encouragement to that individual, but would also maximize the potential of a deepening relationship between your ministry and that person. (Be careful to make personal responses like this via email only if they are received via email. You don't want to upset someone's family members — for example, the non-Christian family member in question — by sending a letter via the postal service after they've privately emailed a request for prayer.)

It is possible, of course, to go much further in an effort to respond to people's prayer needs — particularly given the advances of computer technology. Our agency partner Jack Sheline created a largely automated "variable paragraph library" for the Rex Humbard ministry years ago, which enabled staff members to respond rather specifically to the prayer requests mailed in by donors. Humbard's brief Bible-based observations and prayers regarding various needs common to the human condition — observations and prayers heavy-laden with Scripture — were stored in a database and called up as needed. Today, a ministry team committed to this form of ministry to website visitors could pour their heart and soul into preparing (and frequently updating) such a library and automate the entire system — the ideal use of computerization to enable compassion. Perhaps this idea seems to "go too far" — but how else could a ministry staff, limited in numbers, offer prayer and Bible-based responses to the unlimited number of individuals represented by your website's potential audience?

Could you become comfortable offering a prayer for your website visitors right there *on* a page of your site? Perhaps this approach, too, would fall outside your personal zone of propriety, and that's a valid consideration. But imagine this scenario: Let's say your ministry staff meets once a week, and as part of that meeting, someone leads in prayer, aloud, for the people supporting the ministry financially. What if you recorded that prayer on audio or videotape, transcribed the text of it, and posted it — as text, audio, and/or video — on a page of your website? The prayertime, updated and posted fresh each week, could become one of the most popular pages on your site, simply because of its stunning reality!

Perhaps you could offer website visitors a weekly or monthly "prayer dialogue" or some such, where you initiate an email to them which features some Scripture about prayer, some encouraging words, and an invitation to respond with prayer requests. This could be as elaborate as a weekly (or daily) prayer-related devotional — or as simple as a few lines, written from the heart.

In any case, whenever you email people — even though they have requested it — observe the Internet protocol, or "netiquette," of including a "don't email me about this again" link or option.

It's possible, of course, that some visitors might see your offer of a spiritual partnership with them in a cynical light. But better to have your pure motives misunderstood than to mask them altogether out of fear. Yes, a prayer-bond between your ministry and your website visitors will probably help your ministry as well as your visitors — but that isn't something you should take blame for; it's simply one of the many happy coincidences of people operating according to God's design.

Hope for the Harvesters

Where to go from here?

Forward!

Post a website, if you haven't already. Experiment with your site. Start wherever you are at the moment. Ask questions. Force yourself to open up to new ideas — to the possibility of being wrong sometimes — and to potential of a tremendous new avenue of growth! That's what the Internet represents to your ministry.

God has enormous incentive to help you succeed. Your ministry's exposure on the Internet can become one of the most effective means of fulfilling His Great Commission. Jesus said, in **Mark 16:15**, "Go into all the world" — and that would include the World Wide Web — "and preach the good news to all creation" — which most certainly includes the growing number of Internet surfers! Whatever work God has ordained for your organization to accomplish, that divinely inspired mission can be enhanced by a well designed, highly effective website.

And getting there can be fun. We'll help you if we can. We'd like to!

It would be delightful to say, "We have the Internet all figured out." It just wouldn't be true.

Our agency has a reputation for being highly creative and effective, but conservative with ministries' money. While we innovate, we also want to rely wherever we can on tried-and-true strategies, adapting them creatively — and taking *intelligent* chances when we take chances!

This brand-new thing called the Internet, however,

contradicts the very idea of "tried-and-true." The solution? As we strive to understand the heart of God — the God of the Internet, who *fully* understands it — we find that He graciously honors our efforts, and blesses the work of ministries He has raised up.

God is, quite literally, our only hope — but let's face it: He's the best possible hope we could have. As His servants, and in partnership with Him, we continue to study as hard as we can and learn as much as we can. We take careful notes, as always, and pray earnestly for God's guidance every step of the way. We do our best, and by His grace, our best so far has blessed numerous ministries. But there is way, way more to learn.

So we're on our way.

We would welcome the opportunity to talk with you about growing your ministry to the next level, for the sake of seeing more people come to Christ. Our web address is www.berkeybrendelsheline.com, our email address is servant@berkeybrendelsheline.com, our fax is 330.869.5607, our phone is 330.867.5224, our street address is 60 Shiawassee Avenue, Suite G, Fairlawn, Ohio 44333.

Let's get together and see what God will do!